CONCORDE

By F. G. Clark and Arthur Gibson

This is the first detailed and first-hand account of the most ambitious civil aircraft project ever undertaken – the design, development and manufacture jointly by Britain and France of the Concorde supersonic airliner. F. G. Clark, who wrote the text, and Arthur Gibson, who took the great majority of the photographs which illustrate it, form a team uniquely qualified to present the story of Concorde.
Both have been involved with the project since its inception, Mr Clarke as a member of the staff of British Aircraft Corporation and, before that, Bristol Aircraft Ltd., and Mr Gibson as a consultant designer to BAC and Britain's leading aviation photographer. Both have travelled widely in connection with Concorde's overseas demonstration tours to many different parts of the world.
Their book will surely rank as the authoritative "biography" of one of the most beautiful and exciting aircraft the world has seen.

© 1976 Phoebus Publishing Company/BPC Publishing Limited,
169 Wardour Street, London W1A 2JX. All rights reserved. ISBN 0 7026 0013 X

Published in Australia 1976 by Books for Pleasure, a Division of Paul Hamlyn Pty Limited,
176 South Creek Road, Dee Why West, N.S.W. 2099. ISBN 0 7271 0011 4

Printed in England by Oxley Printing Group. Carlisle, Nottingham, London.

In the whole of Man's history, it is doubtful if there has ever been any field of endeavour in which technological progress has been as swift and as dramatic as in the development of powered flight – progress typified by the two aircraft photographed together, above, at a Paris air show. It is less than 70 years since Louis Blériot's frail little monoplane wrote history by making the world's first international flight, tottering across the narrow waters of the English Channel to its abrupt final landing on English soil. Yet today, the Anglo-French Concorde is making passenger flight at twice the speed of sound across the great oceans of the world a routine reality. In scale and complexity, the Concorde programme is comparable to the U.S.A.'s Apollo Moon-shot programme; as a venture in technological collaboration between two major industrial nations, Concorde is unique.

This is the story of that programme . . .

There were more spectators than usual on the terraces at Orly airport, south of Paris, on that September afternoon in 1973. They had come to see the making of a piece of aviation history – the climax of the fastest-ever Transatlantic crossing by a commercial aircraft.

The plane was the Concorde, built jointly by France and Britain in the most imaginative, most challenging, undertaking in aviation history. Yet the crowd was not enormous, nor was there any feeling of great excitement in the air. The technological "miracle" of yesterday had already been accepted, both in France and in Britain, as a simple fact of life today.

In the countries the aeroplane had just been visiting, the picture had been very different. Ten-mile traffic jams had built up around airports as crowds of a hundred thousand and more gathered to look over the creation that was designed to bring faster-than-sound flight within reach of anyone with the price of a plane ticket.

And, suddenly, there it was, a speck in the eastern sky that grew rapidly. As always, the landing configuration – nose drooped, long undercarriage lowered, the typical high-angle approach of the delta-winged aeroplane – gave it the appearance of a great sea-bird.

The crowd had been told to expect Concorde 02, second of the pre-production aircraft, at 1530. It had come in, in fact, a few minutes ahead of time, landing at Orly only 3hr. 33min. after take-off from Dulles airport, Washington – 213 minutes to cover a distance of nearly 3,900 statute miles. Its average speed had been about 1,100 miles an hour, or about 18 miles a minute.

For 2hr. 16min. the aircraft had flown at Mach 2, about 1,350mph, twice the speed of sound, carrying a payload of 25,000lb., made up of test installations and 32 passengers. In the VIP lounge, newspaper and TV men had gathered to hear about the flight and to interview the crew and passengers, who included airline executives, government officials and aviation journalists.

Jean Franchi and Gilbert Defer, captain and co-pilot (as well as being test pilots of Aérospatiale) were professionally unemotional as they gave the details of what had been, for them, an uneventful flight. The passengers were much more ready to enthuse, and it was to the passengers that Robert Hotz, editor of *Aviation Week* and one of the most experienced journalists present, turned his thoughts.

He wrote: "What is perhaps more important for its (Concorde's) future in airline service is that it has delivered a load of passengers in a remarkably fresh and unfatigued condition that will make them head back toward the 7-8hr. subsonic crossing with the greatest reluctance."

And that is what Concorde is all about – to get the long-distance air traveller there in half the time. Some people feel that this is a reasonable and even laudable objective: others do not. There is nothing new about this fundamental division. There have always been those who wanted to go faster and those who thought the present speed (of ox-cart, stagecoach, sailing ship) was fast enough.

The debate is, however, sterile. Concorde is now already a fact of aviation life. Twenty years ago, Mach 2 was exclusively for super-fit young fighter pilots. Today, thanks to the technological achievement of Concorde, supersonic flight can be placed at the service of sedentary businessmen and the eldest of elder statesmen.

New ideas in aviation nearly always follow a clearly-defined pattern. First comes experimental research; then, if promising, the idea is taken up, at whatever cost, by the armed forces; finally, its reliability, safety and operating economics improve to the point where the application of the new idea to commercial aircraft becomes a practical proposition. In the past, the time gap between first adoption of the innovation by the military and its introduction into airliner service has been around ten years.

It has taken more than twice as long to move from the first supersonic fighters to the entry into service of Concorde and the Soviet Tu 144. The first fighter capable of exceeding Mach 1 in level flight was the F-100 Super Sabre, which entered service in 1953, and by 1958 the Lockheed F-104 had shown itself capable of sustained flight at Mach 2. The time taken to develop a supersonic airliner is no reflection on the design teams, but simply a measure of the magnitude and complexity of the tasks.

It was as early as 1943 that the British government first issued a specification for an experimental transonic aircraft capable of reaching Mach 1.5 (1,000mph) at 36,500ft. By February, 1946, the detail design of this aircraft, the Miles M.52, was nearing completion, but at that point the project was cancelled and substituted by a programme of telemetered transonic flights by air-launched models. It was thought that there was too great an element of risk to the human pilot, and it is worth recalling that later in the same year the famous test pilot Geoffrey de Havilland lost his life when the DH 108 broke up during practice for an attempt on the world speed record.

Perhaps, with hindsight, the decision in 1946 to cancel the M52 can be criticised as having been over-cautious since it handed over to the Americans the lead in supersonic experience. At the time, however, the justification for the decision was the general uncertainty surrounding the aerodynamic and controllability effects of what had come to be known, quite inaccurately, as the "sound barrier."

The phenomenon of the compressibility drag rise which occurs as an aircraft approaches the speed of sound was first examined by the German scientist Adolf Busemann in 1933. Before the advent of the gas turbine engine with its far-greater thrust, it was thought that this sharp increase in drag could well place an upper limit on aircraft speed.

For an appreciation of basic supersonic design philosophy, some understanding of the nature of the compressibility drag problem is necessary. As an aircraft is propelled through the atmosphere by the thrust of its engines, the resistance of the air exerts a force upon it. This force is made up of two components: one is *lift*, which normally acts vertically on the aircraft, and the other is *drag*, acting in a direction opposed to the aircraft's motion. The measure of an aircraft's aerodynamic efficiency is its lift/drag ratio.

When it is moving through the air an aircraft sends out pulses in all directions. As these are sound pulses, their speed is the speed of sound at the altitude at which the aircraft is flying. So long as the aircraft's speed is below the speed of sound, some of these pulses move ahead of the aircraft and give warning to the molecules of air, which rearrange themselves to give the aircraft a relatively unimpeded passage.

But as the aircraft begins to approach the speed of sound, the situation changes radically. No warning pulses can now get ahead of the aircraft, and it has therefore to start forcing its way through the air in much the same way that a ship forces its way through the sea. It has to start compressing the air it meets as it moves forward. The ship creates a bow wave, and the aircraft creates a shock wave cone with its apex at the aircraft nose. Because of the nature of this greatly increased air resistance, there is a corresponding increase in drag (compressibility or "wave drag" as it is sometimes called) and, in the transonic speed range, an inevitable sharp falling-off in aerodynamic efficiency.

The Royal Aircraft Establishment, Farnborough, had been in the forefront of supersonic research in Britain and took the initiative in the discussions leading to the setting up in 1956 of the Supersonic Transport Aircraft Committee, a body which can be fairly claimed to have signposted the way for the future development of supersonic transport in Britain. It had as its chairman the deputy director of RAE, Mr M. B. (later Sir Morien) Morgan, and among its members were some of the best brains in British aviation. It was a truly national committee with representation from the ministries, the airlines and all the important British aircraft and aero-engine companies.

Under the auspices of the STAC, research into various aspects of supersonic transport design was pursued by technical sub-committees. By March, 1959, the work had progressed to a point where the committee was able to report its broad recommendations on the two types of supersonic airliner it thought should be developed. One was a 100-seat aircraft with a cruise speed of Mach 1.2 (800mph) and a maximum range of 1,500 miles. The other was a 150-seat aircraft cruising at Mach 1.8 (1,200-mph) with a Transatlantic range of approximately 3,500 miles.

The British concept
Following receipt of the report, the Ministry of Aviation awarded contracts for the study of various possible configurations for the long-range aircraft. For the time being the medium-range type was put on the shelf, and it was left to the French to revive the proposal for such an aircraft later.

From the wind-tunnel research and theoretical work done under these first feasibility study contracts, it became clear that the slender delta wing planform had advantages over all the other shapes being considered. Furthermore, and contrary to earlier predictions, the aerodynamic efficiency of this planform tended to improve up to about Mach 2.2.

It remained to decide what would be the best fuselage-wing combination to exploit the potential of the delta planform. A joint feasibility study, awarded to Hawker-Siddeley Aviation Ltd. and Bristol Aircraft Ltd., settled the issue. Hawkers investigated a proposal for a fuselage integrated in a wing of deep cross-section while Bristol studied a proposal for a discrete fuselage associated with a thin wing. When the results of the two studies were compared, the "discrete" configuration was found to have definite advantages over the "integrated" version for use in a first-generation supersonic airliner in the size and speed bracket contemplated.

Under a design study contract, BAC proposed the Bristol type 198, a slender delta aircraft similar in configuration to that which Bristol – merged in the newly-formed BAC in 1960 – had made for its feasibility study. It was powered by six Olympus turbojets mounted beneath the wing; it

One of the main BAC design offices. Design studies of supersonic transport began at the BAC factory at Filton (then Bristol Aircraft Ltd.) in the late 1950s.

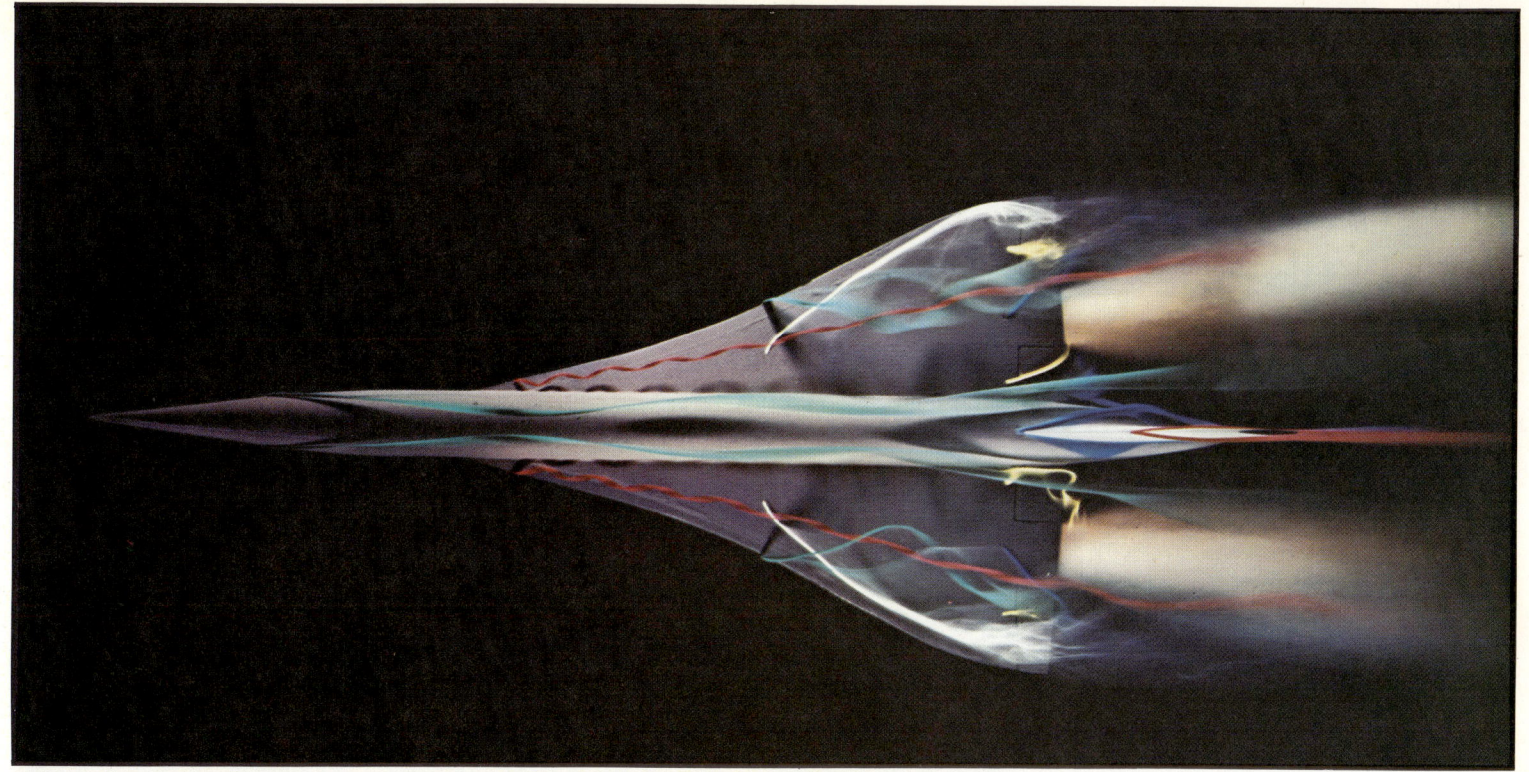

Lofting of Concorde's slender delta wing in progress at the Toulouse factory of Aérospatiale (then Sud Aviation) in the early days of the project.

had a Transatlantic range and a 130-passenger payload; and its maximum take-off weight was about 380,000lb.

Doubts about the weight of the Bristol 198, which increased the intensity of the sonic boom, and reservations about the intake design problems and economics of a six-engine installation, caused the government to call for a proposal for a smaller transport. This was the Bristol Type 223, with four Olympus engines, capable of carrying 100 passengers over a Transatlantic range and with a maximum take-off weight of 250,000lb. This last was an all-British design.

When the design study contract was awarded in 1960, the government made it a condition that BAC should actively explore the possibilities of international collaboration on the project. It was already apparent that there would be heavy demands on finance, manpower, and research and development facilities in developing a supersonic airliner, and there were obvious advantages in sharing the load with another nation if agreement on the basic design principles could be reached.

Approaches were therefore made by BAC to the United States, Germany and France. There was little interest shown in the USA where at that time there was a widespread conviction that the first-generation supersonic civil transport should be based on the Mach 3 B 70 bomber. Germany's reaction was that their industry was not ready to face the challenge of a supersonic airliner just yet and they would require more time to consider such a step.

The intricate patterns of airflow over Concorde's slender delta wingform, revealed by a hydrodynamic tunnel test.

The French concept

French response was very different. Their industry was in good heart and justifiably proud of the Caravelle. Today rear-engined jetliners are accepted as the norm for short- and medium-haul operation, but it was not always so. The Caravelle was the first of the breed and there was much scepticism in Britain and the USA about the configuration before the aircraft proved itself.

France, too, had been investigating the feasibility of developing a supersonic transport, and their thinking had been running on parallel lines to that of the British. The French company Sud-Aviation had a prominent role in this activity. Just as Bristol was merged into BAC, so Sud-Aviation became part of the nationalised SNIAS group, familiarly known as Aérospatiale. It was these two groups that were to become joint airframe contractors for Concorde.

Sud-Aviation and Dassault had already announced that they were concentrating their effort on a medium-range aircraft. The name they gave to their proposal, the Super-Caravelle, was significant, but it was not only their recent Caravelle experience that coloured their thinking. They considered, with some justification, that long range would be a difficult initial design objective for any supersonic transport, and that it would be better to concentrate first on the more easily achievable medium range, extending the range as operating experience was acquired.

The British, on the other hand, were firmly of the view that Transatlantic range was a fundamental requirement for supersonic operation. Whatever the difficulties – and it was accepted that they would be great – it was in the long-range market that the best prospects for a supersonic transport lay, because it was only on sector lengths exceeding 1,500 miles that the time-saving advantages of the higher cruise speed began to show themselves.

When, in accordance with the 1961 design study contract, BAC raised the subject of collaboration with Sud-Aviation, the French company was quite prepared for serious discussions, but on the basis that there would be two different types of aircraft. Later in 1961, BAC and Sud-Aviation each put in proposals for long-range and medium-range aircraft, but these still showed the differences in the approach to key design problems. By this time, there had also been direct consultation between the French and British governments on the subject and the companies' proposals did not go far enough to meet the governments' wish for joint working.

The Anglo-French compromise
The leaders of the two design teams had been in regular consultation, however, and were gradually coming to a closer understanding of the others' viewpoint and motivation. This steady movement towards an agreement was a long, and sometimes wearing, process, but it helped to lay the foundation for the years of joint working that lay ahead.

By the Farnborough Air Show in September, 1962, agreement was so close that a model of the proposed aircraft was shown on the BAC stand. This attracted much Press and public attention, and there was some speculation that the expected Anglo-French agreement to build an SST (supersonic transport) might be announced. But there were still two months to wait.

The four men who had been most closely concerned with the direction of the joint design studies and discussions were, on the British side, Dr A. E. (later Sir Archibald) Russell, technical director of BAC's Filton Division, and Dr W. J. Strang, chief engineer of Filton Division and, on the

French side, Pierre Satre and Lucien Servanty, technical director and chief engineer respectively of Sud-Aviation. Each of the four was an aeronautical engineer of international standing.

In October in a small office in Paris, a final move was made in the protracted negotiations. Bill Strang and Lucien Servanty were closeted for a whole day, with a single draughtsman and drawing board, and instructed to come out with a common three-view general arrangement drawing for the long-range and medium-range aircraft. They succeeded, although it would be hard to imagine two men more unlike in temperament, background and personality. Lucien Servanty was a forceful and fiery character, who did not suffer fools gladly. Bill Strang is an equable, quiet-spoken man, who leads rather than drives his team. They were, one might have thought, a fairly unlikely pair to work together as collaborators on the most difficult technological project ever tackled in Europe.

Yet this partnership, like many others in the Concorde organisation, grew and flourished on the firm basis of mutual respect for the other's intellect and integrity. When Servanty died in 1973, soon after 02 had made the first Concorde non-stop crossing of the North Atlantic, Bill Strang wrote in *Flight International*:

"Lucien Servanty was, above all, a dedicated engineer. He combined a wide intellectual grasp of his subject with a great capacity for absorbing detail. Setbacks never daunted him. They were accepted as a challenge and always his first step was to analyse the situation in depth in order to isolate the underlying causes of the problem.

"Once he had made up his mind, he was prepared to support his opinions vigorously,

A Concorde that could never fly – the full-scale wooden mock-up at Filton, used mainly for three-dimensional representation of seating, galley and other interior arrangements.

deploying an impassioned array of arguments. He was always a loyal friend and ally. Sometimes we were together against 'the rest.' Sometimes we were ourselves in disagreement, and I believe a partnership such as ours would have been of little value if this had not happened from time to time. But however tough the in-fighting, as soon as we left the office Lucien would at once become the charming and cultivated host I knew so well."

The joint proposal which finally emerged from the inter-company discussions was for a slender-delta-winged monoplane, with common dimensions but different internal layouts for the medium- and the long-range versions. The medium-range aircraft was to seat 100 passengers and would take-off at a maximum of 220,000lb., and the long-range had a capacity of 90 passengers and an all-up weight of 262,000lb.

A review was made of the design, production and research facilities available for the joint project, and general agreement was reached on the allocation of responsibilities between the two companies. At last, on November 29, 1962, an agreement was signed in London by Julian Amery, Minister of Supply, and Geoffroy de Courcel, the French Ambassador to Britain, by which the two governments undertook to finance the development and building of a supersonic airliner. Everything would be shared – costs, work, and proceeds of sales.

Before the signing of the treaty, BAC and Sud-Aviation had agreed in principle on how the work of developing and pro-

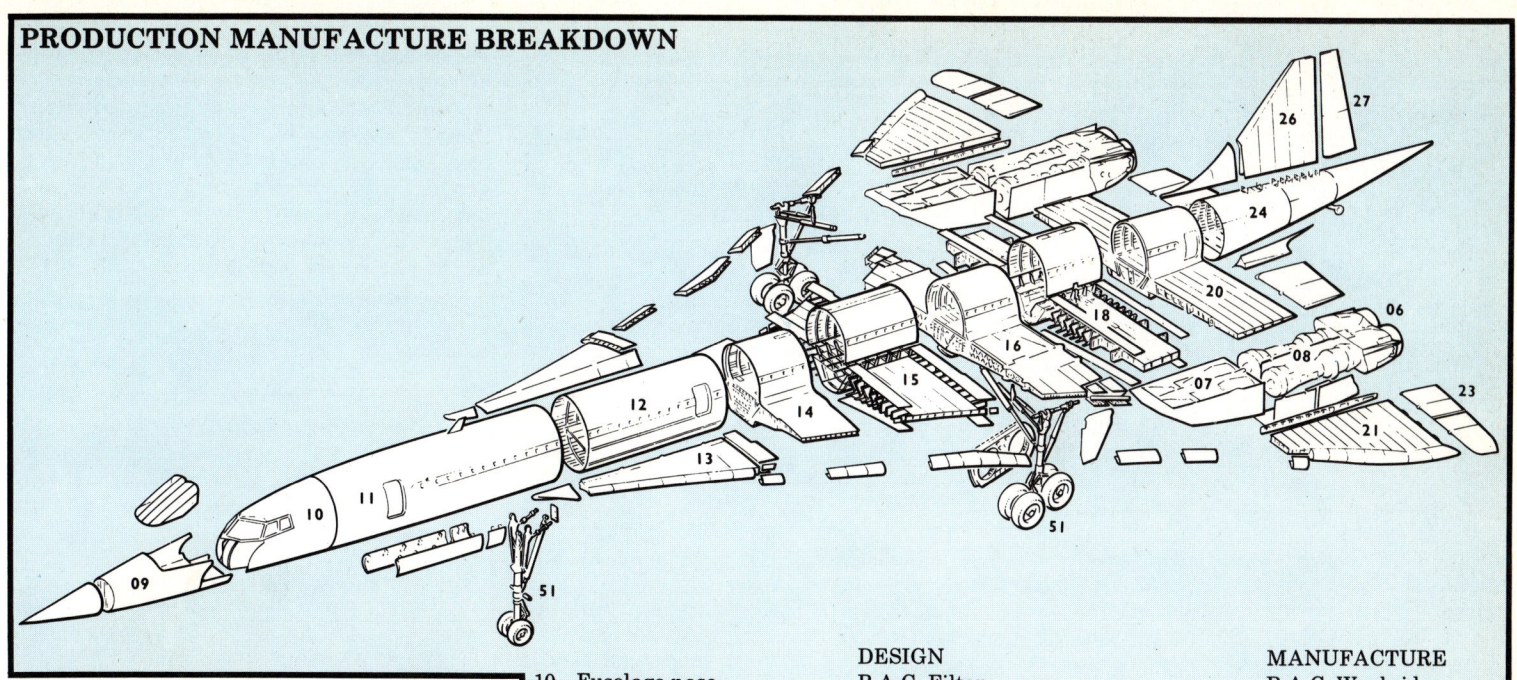

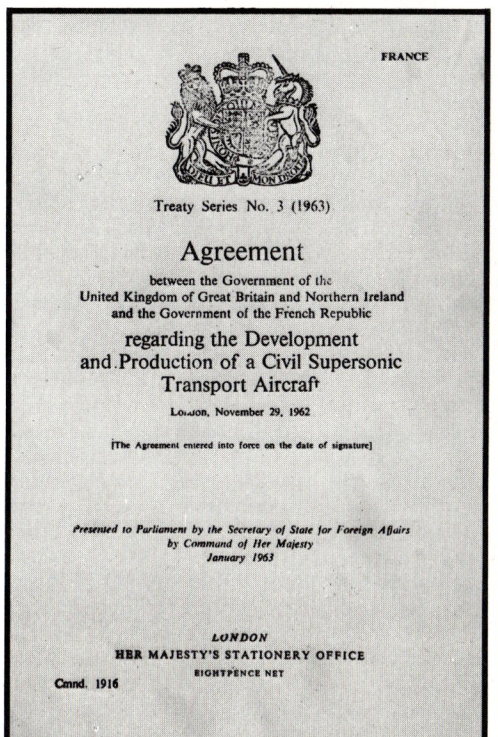

Below: Concorde's "birth certificate" – front cover of the government paper recording the 1962 Anglo-French agreement to embark on the programme.

FRANCE

Treaty Series No. 3 (1963)

Agreement

between the Government of the
United Kingdom of Great Britain and Northern Ireland
and the Government of the French Republic

regarding the Development
and Production of a Civil Supersonic
Transport Aircraft

London, November 29, 1962

[The Agreement entered into force on the date of signature]

Presented to Parliament by the Secretary of State for Foreign Affairs
by Command of Her Majesty
January 1963

LONDON
HER MAJESTY'S STATIONERY OFFICE
EIGHTPENCE NET

Cmnd. 1916

		DESIGN	MANUFACTURE
10	Fuselage nose	B.A.C. Filton	B.A.C. Weybridge
09	Droop nose	Marshalls	Marshalls/Hurn
11	Forward fuselage	B.A.C. Filton	B.A.C. Weybridge
24	Rear fuselage	B.A.C. Weybridge	B.A.C. Weybridge
26	Fin	B.A.C. Weybridge	B.A.C. Weybridge
27	Rudder	B.A.C. Weybridge	B.A.C. Weybridge
25	Nacelles *comprising* :		
07	Air intake	B.A.C. Filton	B.A.C. Filton
08	Engine bay	B.A.C. Filton	B.A.C. Filton
06	Nozzles	SNECMA	SNECMA
—	Engines	Rolls Royce – Bristol	Rolls Royce – Bristol
12	Intermediate fuselage	B.A.C. Filton	S.N.I.A.S. Marignane
14	Centre wing	S.N.I.A.S. Toulouse + H. Dubois	S.N.I.A.S. Marignane
13	Forward wing	S.N.I.A.S. Suresnes	S.N.I.A.S. Bouguenais
15	Centre wing	S.N.I.A.S. Suresnes + La Courneuve	S.N.I.A.S. Bouguenais
16	Centre wing	S.N.I.A.S. Toulouse	S.N.I.A.S. Toulouse
18	Centre wing	S.N.I.A.S. Toulouse	S.N.I.A.S. Toulouse
23	Elevons	S.N.I.A.S. Suresnes	S.N.I.A.S. Toulouse
20	Centre wing	S.N.I.A.S. Toulouse + Fiat	S.N.I.A.S. St. Nazaire
21	Outer wing	AMD Dassault	AMD Dassault/Bourges
51	Landing gear main	Hispano Suiza	Hispano Suiza
51	Landing gear nose	Messier	Messier

ducing the airframe of the supersonic airliner should be shared between them. One of the companies' first tasks now was to convert this general understanding into a definitive agreement. They had to produce an acceptable and practical plan for enabling the design and production work to be broken down and allocated, on a 60–40 split to France and Britain. It took long meetings and much hard bargaining to agree on a manufacturing break-down but, in general, the division of responsibilities then formulated still holds good today.

The airframe work was divided 60–40 in favour of France because the balance of work on the engine was weighted in favour of Britain. By November, 1962, the engine selected for the Concorde, the supersonic version of the Bristol-Siddeley Olympus, was already being developed. Engines were in existence and running on the test-bed, and whatever adjustments might be made in the new programme to allow joint Anglo-French development of the Olympus 593, the British work content would be greater than the French.

Agreement on the airframe breakdown enabled BAC and Sud-Aviation to begin the allocation of work within their own groups. Each of the factories concerned was given full responsibility for detail design and manufacture of the component or components allocated to it. The BAC factories which received Concorde sub-assembly work were Weybridge, Filton, Hurn and Preston; the Sud-Aviation factories were St Martin, Toulouse, Bouguenais, St Nazaire and Bourges.

Plans were also made for two final assembly lines to be established, one in Britain and the other in France. In series production, the odd-numbered Concordes are assembled in the St Martin plant at Toulouse, and the even-numbered at the Filton works of BAC. There is, however, no duplication at the sub-assembly stage. For example, all the nose fuselages (Sections 10 and 11) are built at Weybridge; all the centre fuselage-wing components (Section 14) are produced at Marignane.

In structural design, BAC was made responsible for the front fuselage including the flight deck, the engine nacelles, air intakes and engine mountings, the rear fuselage, fin and rudder. It had design responsibility as well for the following systems: electrics, oxygen, fuel, engine instrumentation, engine controls, fire, air conditioning distribution and de-icing. Sud-Aviation's share of the structure comprised the entire centre fuselage section, the wings including elevons, and the landing gear. The French company was also given design responsibility for the hydraulics, flying control, navigation, radio and air-conditioning supply systems.

Working together

With this clearly-defined division of overall responsibilities and the firm allocation of sub-assembly responsibilities, work could be started across a wide front. Numbers of people deployed on the project increased steadily until the total, including those employed by sub-contractors and suppliers, reached nearly 50,000. Most of these thousands were able to get on with their work without reference to anyone except their immediate superiors. But their efforts could only be effective so long as there was co-ordinated direction at the top and close liaison at all executive levels throughout the international organisation. This organ-

Left: In November, 1962, the supersonic version of the Olympus turbojet was already running on the test-beds. Below: The Concorde programme was made possible because a few score pairs of people learned how to work together at the factories and offices on each side of the English Channel. Right: The two Concorde prototypes in the air at the Paris Air Show in 1969.

isation has worked well because a few scores of *pairs* of people, French and British, learned to work in partnership.

Without firm handling, one aspect of the collaboration arrangements could have been a source of serious friction. Although it was never precisely defined, there was a general understanding that Sud should lead on the design side of the project and that BAC should be leaders on the manufacturing side. But the first few months' working together made it clear that joint direction would be necessary. Therefore, the two leaders of the project, General André Puget, President of Sud-Aviation, and Sir George Edwards, chairman of BAC, who held the chairmanship of the Aircraft Committee of Directors in rotation for several years, decided to take all major executive decisions jointly, having talked out the problem between them. On paper, the committee had a chairman and a vice-chairman; in practice, it had two chairmen.

Intervention at chairman level was not often required. Indeed, Sir George has suggested dryly that one of the secrets of the success of the Concorde industrial collaboration was that the Committee of Directors did not meet very often. In contrast, other Anglo-French pairs at executive level needed to keep in daily contact by executive aircraft, telephone, telex or data link. In many cases, collaboration led to firm friendships.

There were, of course, incompatibilities and friction. Two large independent engineering organisations, each jealously proud – with good reason – of its reputation and skill, were being compelled to join forces on a project for which both had done much spadework. Some of them thought of it as a shotgun marriage. There were bound to be personality problems, but that would have been equally true had BAC been working with another British company or Sud with another French one.

The language barrier
Undoubtedly, some· of the problems of professional pride were exacerbated by language difficulties and by differences in national temperament. Early meetings on any subject tended to divide on purely national lines, but in the long run nationality factors played a surprisingly small part. Men who worked through the "running-in" period of the collaboration are often asked how the problem of the language barrier was overcome. Their reply is usually on the lines that, if you could not find a way round the barrier, you just barged through it.

Because Sud-Aviation had been building Caravelles for the international market, many of their engineering and sales executives spoke good English, and that gave them a head start over their British opposite numbers whose French was, in the main, at the rusty sixth-form standard. A number of BAC men have since acquired a working knowledge of French, however, particularly in their professional field, so that many meetings can be conducted bilingually, with the French and the British speaking in their own language without immediate translation.

One British custom which never ceased to bemuse the French is the ready use of Christian names. This was underlined at the end of a meeting at which agreement had been reached on a specially complicated point. The leader of the British group said: "Jean, just so that both sides are clear on what has been agreed, why not get Honorine in and dictate a note on the subject?" The Frenchman replied: *"D'accord, mais qui est Honorine?"*

Honorine was his own secretary, but, although she had worked for him for three years, her French chief still knew her as "Mademoiselle Dupont."

Double standards
As the project moved onwards, more and more people in both countries grew convinced on two points – that Concorde was well worthwhile, and that Britain and France had a much better chance of seeing the programme through to success by working together than by going it alone. At bottom, it was the strength of these convictions that enabled the Concorde team to push doggedly ahead through all the crises and vicissitudes of the decade that followed.

One technical question frequently asked is: What happens about the two standards of measurements in France and Britain? The simple solution to this problem was to allow both sides to work in the scales to which they are accustomed. A common system of numbering engineering drawings was established before manufacture of the prototype aircraft began. French drawings were dimensioned in metric measurements, and British drawings in feet and inches. At interface points in the structure, the relevant drawings were dimensioned in both scales.

A minor, but not unimportant, requirement was to find a suitable name for the aircraft. When the collaboration began, the design was being referred to by the British as the "SST" or the "223," a reference to the Bristol type number. Neither title could be regarded as inspired or inspiring. The French used the terms "TSS" (*transport supersonique*) or, quite frequently, "Super-Caravelle." There were those in Britain who felt that they could not accept the implications of the latter name.

One Sunday afternoon in January, 1963, the suggestion that the aircraft should be called "Concorde" emerged from an informal family conference in the home of a BAC executive. It was arrived at by the simple process of thumbing through *Roget's Thesaurus*. At this family discussion, the first reaction to the suggestion of "Concorde" was the question: "With the 'e,' of course?" To which the answer was: "Yes."

When the suggestion was put forward officially, the British side approved it tentatively and then submitted it to the French. There were some preliminary murmurs of approval but the subject was regarded as a matter for decision by "higher authority." It is ironic that the first indication that the name had been officially adopted in France came in the famous speech by General de Gaulle in which he dashed Britain's hopes of joining the Common Market. In it, the French President mentioned "the Concorde supersonic airliner" and said there was no reason why this kind of scientific and industrial collaboration between the countries of the Six and Britain should not continue.

So the project had a name. Or, rather, it had two names for the British government soon decreed that in this country the spelling "Concord" should be used. This trifling difference proved to be a small but recurring source of friction for several years. But at the roll-out of the first Concorde prototype at Toulouse in December, 1967, Mr Anthony Wedgwood Benn, then British Minister of Technology, finally resolved what he described as the only disagreement with France that had occurred during the years of co-operation on the project. He had decided, he said, that the British "Concorde" should from now on also be written with an "e."

When, in November, 1962, the British and French governments agreed to develop and build a supersonic airliner, they and the manufacturers knew that there would have to be an exhaustive research and development programme before the aircraft could be certificated for passenger operation. Even those closest to the project did not at that time foresee the full scale, complexity and cost of this programme.

The Concorde engineering team was working on the frontiers of technical knowledge and preparing to venture into areas not hitherto explored by commercial aircraft designers. They could not know where their research would lead them or what unpredictable problems might be ahead. In the event, the Concorde test programme was to require more than a decade of research on the ground and nearly 5,000 hours of flight development,

by far the most thorough and comprehensive programme ever mounted in support of a civil aircraft type.

In the earlier years of the programme, the research effort was concentrated principally in aerodynamics, materials and structures. While this was going on, the engineering organisation faced up to the difficult task of formulating a preliminary aircraft design, sufficiently detailed to enable marketing discussions with potential customers to be started.

Aerodynamics and materials

Every supersonic aircraft design presents the aerodynamicist with a range of difficult problems, including two which are of supreme importance. One is the aerodynamic aspects of the powerplant installation. Propulsive efficiency is a critical factor in subsonic aircraft design, but it is

even more crucial to the success of a supersonic aircraft and more difficult to achieve because of the widely varying airflow demands of the engine in different phases of a supersonic mission.

The second challenge arises, not from a specific installation, but the total airframe configuration. To meet it the aerodynamicist has to produce a satisfactory compromise between two inherently conflicting requirements: the need for minimum drag in supersonic flight and the need for controllability and ease of handling in subsonic flight, particularly in landing and take-off. Trim tabs, spoilers and other external moving surfaces used in subsonic aircraft control cannot be utilised in a supersonic airliner design since they would cause unacceptable drag.

These considerations had a profound influence on the adoption of a long stream-

decision closely linked to the choice of Mach 2 as the design cruise speed. This policy was ultimately to prove a sound one, but it could be implemented only after a painstaking evaluation of available aluminium alloys. For this purpose, many thousands of specimens were tested for mechanical properties, fatigue strength, and resistance to corrosion.

A new requirement, directly related to supersonic operation, involved testing for resistance to *creep*, the name that engineers give to the deformation of metal caused by interaction between mechanical loadings and high temperatures. Creep was a phenomenon familiar to the aero-engine designer, but something new to the airframe man. To check possible materials for creep-resistance, samples were submitted to long periods of round-the-clock testing in specially-designed, automatically-controlled installations.

Finally, the choice was made of a copper-based aluminium alloy, known in Britain as RR58 and in France as AU2GN. This alloy had originally been developed for use in gas turbine blades, but the suppliers were able to give assurances that it could be produced in whatever form – sheet, billet,

A massive ground testing programme has been carried out – and some tests will continue far ahead into Concorde's career in airline service. Proving the basic configuration of the aircraft involved over 5,000 hours of wind tunnel testing (above). The main structural test programmes have been carried out on special rigs at RAE Farnborough (right), which is responsible for fatigue testing, and (opposite) at CEAT, Toulouse, where static tests began in September, 1969.

lined fuselage and slender delta wing as the basic Concorde configuration. Proving the validity of this aerodynamic shape required 5,000 hours of studies in subsonic, transonic and supersonic wind-tunnels, supported by large-capacity computers and much research. From this long process, the original design emerged refined and enlarged, but not fundamentally changed.

Ground studies, backed by later flight experience, fully vindicated the earlier decision to avoid any form of variable-geometry wing as a means of achieving the supersonic-subsonic performance compromise. In supersonic military aircraft design, where operational economics is of secondary importance, the "swing wing" is a favoured solution to this problem. In the present state of the art, however, the weight and complexity of the swing wing hinge mechanism rule it out for commercial operation.

Between the prototype design stage and the final definition of the entry-into-service standard aircraft, various configuration changes were introduced, mainly in the areas of the nose and visor, the wing and the rear fuselage. On Concorde, the visor is the retractable upper section of the nose fuselage. This is lowered for maximum forward visibility at landing and take-off and raised in supersonic flight to streamline the nose and protect the flight deck transparencies against heat and pressure. On the prototypes, the visor was of aluminium alloy construction, with cut-outs affording a limited degree of forward vision when the visor was raised. It was never expected that

such an arrangement would be acceptable either to certification authorities or to airline pilots, but it was adopted as an interim measure pending further aerodynamic testing and predictable advances in glass technology. The fully glazed visor, introduced on the pre-production aircraft and now standardised, provides excellent flight deck visibility.

In flight, the Concorde wing looks beautiful – and beautifully simple. At closer quarters it can be seen for what it is: a most complex aerodynamic form, with a precisely-calculated degree of camber and taper across the wing structure itself and a combination of droop and twist along the leading edge. Camber, taper, droop, and twist all make their contribution to Concorde's good handling characteristics at low speed without prejudicing its supersonic performance. Much of the later stages of the aerodynamic research programme was devoted to detail refinements in outer camber, the wing tips and the leading edge.

In the fuselage, the major configuration change was the extension and re-shaping of the tail section. Compared with the prototypes, the upper line of the fuselage extends further beyond the fin and now runs almost horizontally, and the lower line sweeps up to meet it at the tail. This change had a significant effect in reducing supersonic drag and provided a bonus in increased fuel capacity.

One of the initial Concorde design decisions was the selection of aluminium alloy as the basic structural material, a

forging – and to whatever unit size the Concorde design might require.

The many other types of material used in Concorde have all had to be rigorously tested to prove their suitability for application in a supersonic airliner. They include the titanium, stainless steel, and Inconel components used in the engine bays, the glazings in the flight deck and cabin windows, and a variety of plastics, paints, sealants, adhesives, and non-ferrous materials.

Exhaustive tests

With the material selection made, the way was clear to start on the planned programme of structural research. Once again, the facts of supersonic life introduced new complications into the test programme. To have any real value, the laboratory tests needed to reproduce the thermal profile of a typical supersonic flight; the sudden rise in skin temperature during acceleration into the supersonic regime, the heat soak during supersonic cruise, and the sudden cooling of the aircraft surface during deceleration to subsonic speed.

The whole Concorde structural programme culminated in the testing of two complete airframes in vast new laboratories built with this objective in view. One airframe was subjected to static load testing at CEAT, Toulouse, and the second is undergoing fatigue testing in the structures laboratory at the Royal Aircraft Establishment, Farnborough.

Static testing of the airframe at CEAT began in September, 1969, the first phase of the programme being the imposition of progressive design loads at room temperatures. When the structure had been cleared in these conditions, the tests were repeated in transient and steady temperature conditions representative of actual in-flight operation. An impression of the scale of the test may be gained from the following statistics: 80 servo-controlled hydraulic jacks impose the test loads; kinetic heating simulation is provided by 35,000 infra-red lamps; 70,000 litres of liquid nitrogen are used for cooling, making possible a reduction in skin temperature from +120°C to −10°C within 15 minutes; and the test instrumentation is capable of recording and processing 8,000 data points every two seconds.

The test programme was successfully completed in 1972 and, as a result, the airframe was cleared for 385,000lb. take-off weight. Since that time, further static testing has cleared the structure to a take-off weight of 400,000lb.

Static testing proves the integrity of an airframe structure in relation to the numerous transient heavy loadings, aerodynamic and mechanical, to which it will be submitted in flight conditions. It is essential to complement these tests by a thorough appraisal of the fatigue life of the airframe; in other words, its ability to sustain, year in and year out, the regularly-repeated cycle of loadings imposed in the course of a normal flight. Fatigue testing of the Concorde airframe is thought to be the most elaborate exercise of its kind ever attempted.

In the RAE laboratory, the fatigue test specimen is encased in a kind of outer "glove", providing an annular duct around the airframe through which hot and cold air is pumped to reproduce the flight temperature cycle. Hot water is used for heating the air and refrigerated ammonia liquid for cooling it. Circulation is by means of five 2,300hp motor-fans. A hundred servo-controlled hydraulic jacks are employed for external loading of the specimen, and internal loads – representing cabin

pressurisation and air conditioning and fuel movement – are also imposed.

To reduce fatigue test time, internal heating and cooling of the specimen have been provided, and maximum temperatures applied are at a higher level (120°C against 100°C) than those encountered in flight. It had been established in earlier tests that the fatigue effects of a *soak* at a given temperature for a given period of time can be exactly reproduced in a shorter period at a higher temperature. The effects of a one-hour cycle on the RAE rig are therefore equivalent to those of a typical three-hour flight.

Fatigue testing started in August, 1973, and by the end of 1974, the certification requirement of 6,800 cycles had been met. For some years to come, it is planned to complete 7,000 flight cycles yearly which will mean that the test specimen will always have built up at least three times as much fatigue life as the earliest aircraft to enter passenger service.

A variety of other tests has been made on different parts of the structure. For example, development work on the flight deck and cabin glazings included static test to failure, fatigue cycling under realistic temperature conditions, and fail-safe testing in which one element of the glazing has been deliberately failed while the remainder is under load. Cockpit windows have been subjected to bird impact tests, and the whole structure to hail impact tests. An important feature of the programme was acoustic fatigue testing in France and Britain to establish the resistance of the tail and fin structure to the high-jet-noise environment.

Like the aircraft structure, all the Concorde systems had to be designed to oper-

ate over the much wider range of temperatures that supersonic operation involves. These systems have been individually tested and developed in specially constructed full-scale ground test rigs, many of which are impressive engineering achievements in their own right. There are major test installations for the following systems; hydraulics, electrics, flying controls, fuel management, powerplant, undercarriage, and air conditioning. Use of these rigs enabled many systems design problems to be ironed out before the prototypes flew and thus saved much valuable flight development time.

The hydraulics rig is at Aérospatiale's Blagnac, Toulouse, design centre and is a complete replica of the flying control system with the associated hydraulic and electrical systems. It also incorporates the undercarriage functioning system. Adjoining this rig is the Concorde design flight simulator, one of the most advanced installations of its kind in the world. Provision is made for the hydraulics rig to be connected to the simulator flight deck for testing of the flight control system.

Although the simulator has been used to some extent for flight crew training, it is primarily a design tool. Before flight testing began, it was extensively used for investigation of flying characteristics and studies of control-system response, and it has been linked to Air Traffic Control at Orly airport, Paris, to enable ATC authorities to study techniques of integrating supersonic airliners into the existing operational patterns. At the Filton works of BAC there is a simpler form of flight simulator employed for the study of specific design cases.

Also at Filton is the massive fuel systems test rig, which consists basically of a mov-

This fuel systems test rig at Filton was built to provide an accurate simulation of all flight attitudes and accelerations the aircraft would encounter up to an altitude of 65,000 ft.

able platform on which is mounted a complete reproduction of the aircraft's fuel tank system. During a test cycle, the platform is moved to simulate the attitudes and accelerations that the aircraft will experience in flight, and at the actual fuel temperatures and pressures and rates of climb and descent. Use of this rig enabled modifications of the fuel management system to be introduced early in the programme.

Two full-scale rigs were built for electrical systems testing, one for the generation system and the other for the distribution system. There are other important systems rigs, notably those for the engine air intake system, and for undercarriage, wheels, and brakes. Nobody has ever seriously disputed the makers' claims that, when it goes into airline service, Concorde will be the most thoroughly-tested airliner in aviation history.

Producing the power

Concorde's cruise speed of 1,350mph is equivalent to the muzzle velocity of a .303 rifle bullet. The objective was to design and build a passenger aircraft capable of maintaining this speed for more than two hours at a time. One of the most important problems facing the designers was therefore to produce a powerplant capable of achieving this level of performance.

Payload represents about seven per cent of the total take-off weight of a supersonic transport whereas a typical modern subsonic airliner can carry about 24 per cent

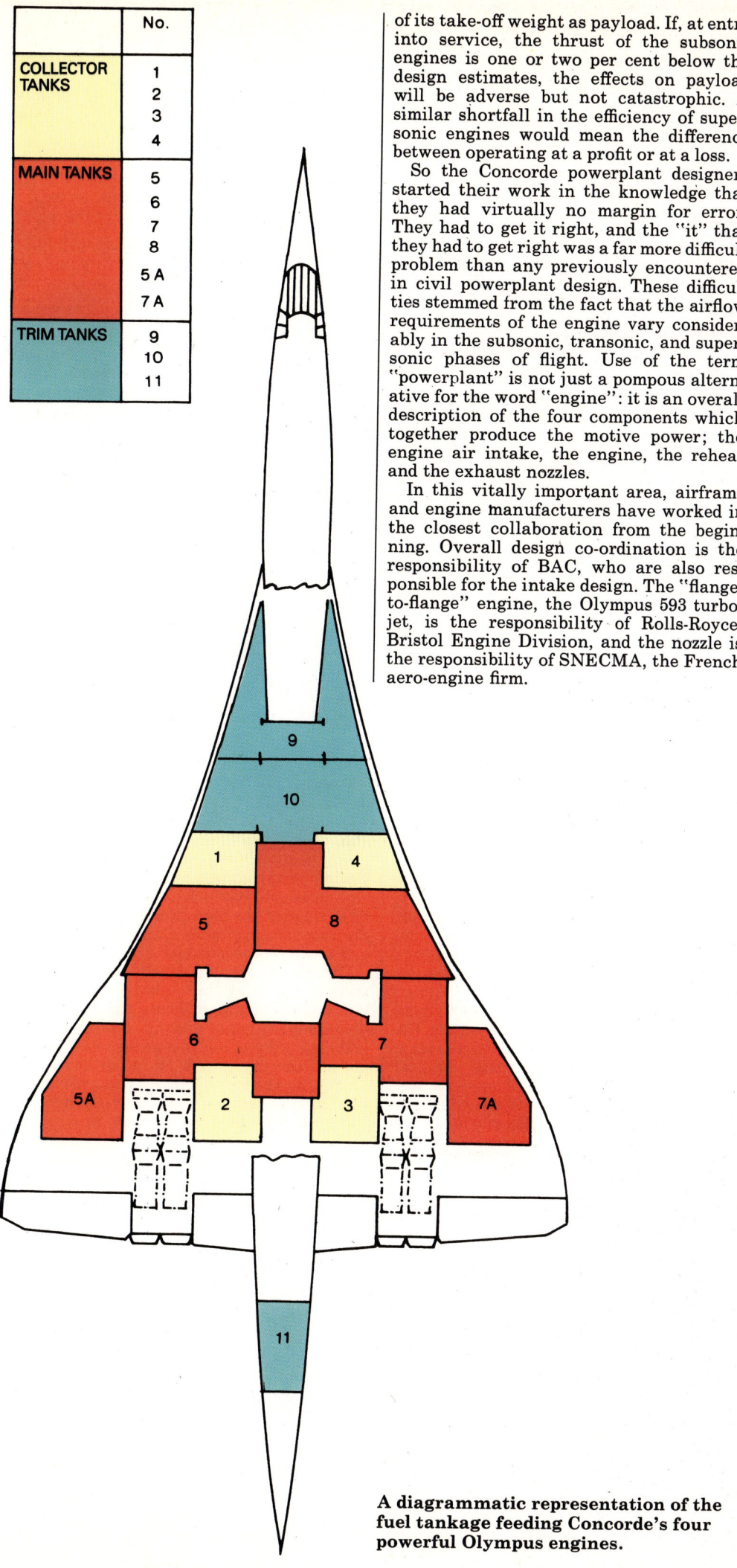

	No.
COLLECTOR TANKS	1
	2
	3
	4
MAIN TANKS	5
	6
	7
	8
	5 A
	7 A
TRIM TANKS	9
	10
	11

A diagrammatic representation of the fuel tankage feeding Concorde's four powerful Olympus engines.

of its take-off weight as payload. If, at entry into service, the thrust of the subsonic engines is one or two per cent below the design estimates, the effects on payload will be adverse but not catastrophic. A similar shortfall in the efficiency of supersonic engines would mean the difference between operating at a profit or at a loss.

So the Concorde powerplant designers started their work in the knowledge that they had virtually no margin for error. They had to get it right, and the "it" that they had to get right was a far more difficult problem than any previously encountered in civil powerplant design. These difficulties stemmed from the fact that the airflow requirements of the engine vary considerably in the subsonic, transonic, and supersonic phases of flight. Use of the term "powerplant" is not just a pompous alternative for the word "engine": it is an overall description of the four components which together produce the motive power; the engine air intake, the engine, the reheat and the exhaust nozzles.

In this vitally important area, airframe and engine manufacturers have worked in the closest collaboration from the beginning. Overall design co-ordination is the responsibility of BAC, who are also responsible for the intake design. The "flange-to-flange" engine, the Olympus 593 turbojet, is the responsibility of Rolls-Royce, Bristol Engine Division, and the nozzle is the responsibility of SNECMA, the French aero-engine firm.

In a gas turbine engine, air is drawn in through an intake and is compressed (and therefore heated) by a compressor driven by a turbine at the rear of the engine. The hot compressed air passes into a combustion chamber where fuel is injected into it, the fuel-air mixture is ignited and the hot gases are ejected through the rear jet pipe to provide forward thrust. Between the combustion chamber and the jet pipe, the exhaust gases also drive the turbine.

The Olympus engine

The Olympus used in Concorde is a twin-spool turbojet, which is almost equivalent to saying that it is two engines in one, since it has two independent compressors each linked to its own turbine. This design concept was first evolved in Bristol some 25 years ago to meet the engine requirement for the subsonic military aircraft known later as the Vulcan bomber.

Harking back to basic principles, it is clear that if compression of the intake air can be increased, its temperature will rise and less fuel will be needed to produce an equivalent amount of thrust energy. To achieve a higher compression ratio, the Olympus designers adopted the novel solution of using a low pressure and a high pressure compressor running in series.

The Olympus engine is much older than Concorde. In the course of flight development of the first mark of Olympus, a Canberra aircraft, powered with two of the engines, broke the world altitude record as long ago as 1953. The Olympus-powered Vulcan began RAF service in 1956, and the engine thrust was steadily increased from the 11,000lb. of the Mk 101 up to 20,000lb. for the Mk 301.

But the evolution of the Olympus still had a long way to go, and the next step forward was to take it across the border from subsonic to supersonic. A supersonic engine, later designated the Olympus 320, was developed for the BAC TSR2 military aircraft (the initials standing for "Tactical Strike Reconnaissance"), and, although there was no departure from the twin-spool design concept, changes were made in materials to meet the higher operating temperatures.

The first TSR2 made its maiden flight in September, 1964, and a second was nearing readiness for flight when, in April, 1965, the British government decided to cancel the project. Britain was left, however, with a technological legacy in the form of a supersonic turbojet engine.

The clinching point when it came to a choice of engine for Europe's supersonic transport was not just the record of the Olympus, but its *availability*. Other contenders were still at the drawing-board stage, but the Olympus 320 had been built, had run on the test-bed, and had flown, first in a Vulcan flying test-bed and then in the TSR2 itself. A detailed account of the subsequent development of the 593 would almost fill a book. Possibly the best way to sum up the remarkable progress that has been made since the inception of the Olympus, is to contrast thrust figures: the Olympus 100 first ran at 9,140lb. thrust and the Olympus 593 has demonstrated a thrust of over 40,000lb. – equal to the total brake-horsepower of 10,000 Minis.

One Olympus development must be singled out for special mention. The two prototype Concordes were powered with early versions of the Olympus 593B, which

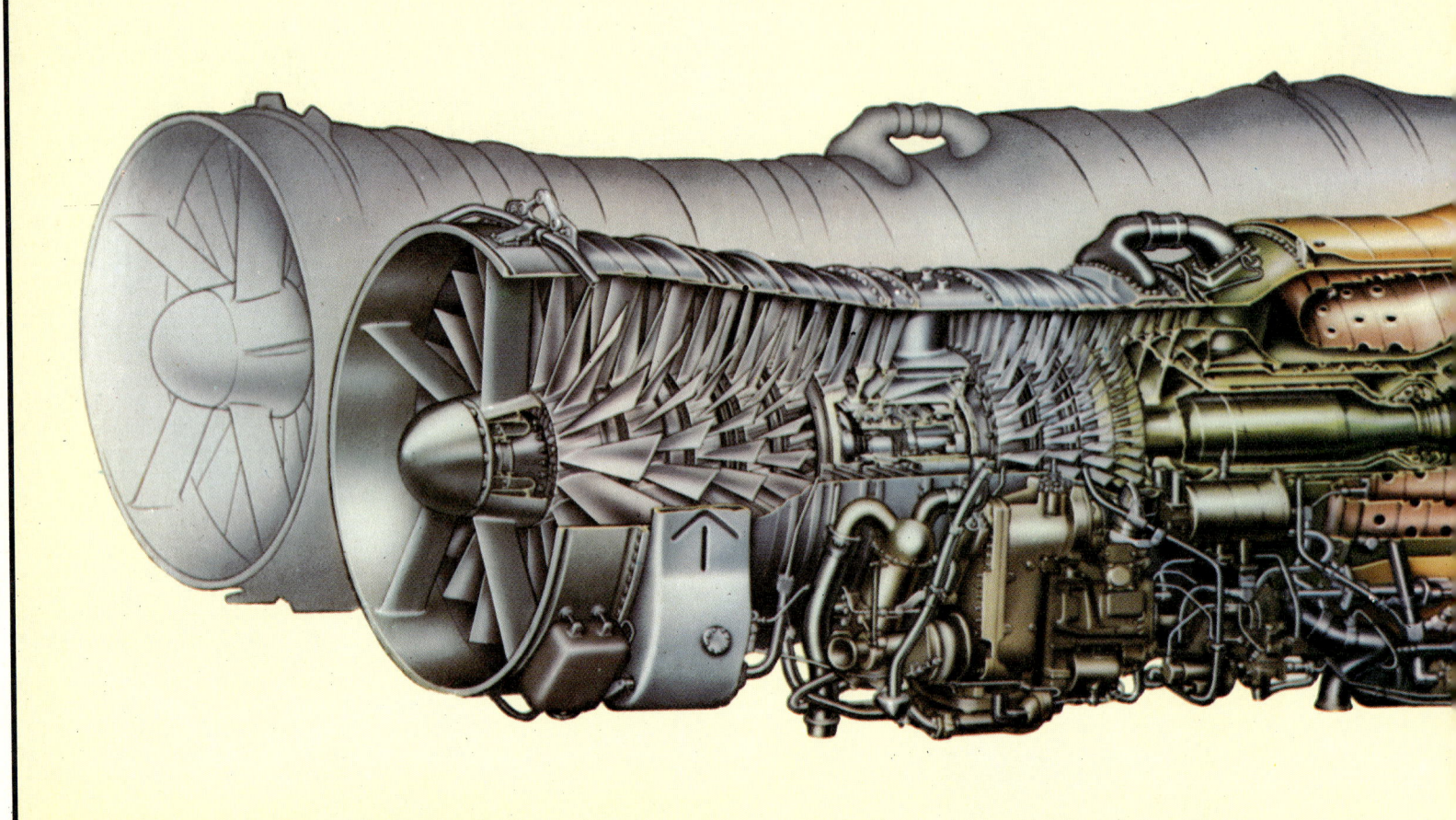

produced much smoke at take-off and landing. To meet the criticism about the exhaust trails Rolls-Royce and SNECMA decided in 1969 to develop for the Olympus a type of combustion chamber which had already demonstrated, in the Viper, Sapphire and Pegasus engines, its ability to eliminate smoke. The introduction of this "annular" type combustion chamber, in conjunction with a new vaporising fuel injector system, has made the Concorde exhaust virtually smoke-free. In this respect Concorde ranks among the cleanest of current aircraft.

Supersonic flight brings the airframe designer new problems because of the increased structure temperatures it creates; it brings the engine designer new problems because of the higher operating temperatures required to produce the higher thrust. At Mach 2 air will enter the intake at about −60°C, will be compressed in the intake and be at about 130°C when it reaches the face of the engine, and will leave the high-pressure compressor at 550°C.

In order to cope with these extremely high temperatures, materials used in the subsonic Olympus have been superseded. The low-pressure compressor and the first stages of the high-pressure compressor are made in titanium; this not only saves weight but is robust enough to withstand ice, birds and other "foreign objects" that get ingested into the engine. To resist the even higher temperatures further back in the engine, nickel-based alloys are used for the final stage of the high-pressure compressor, the combustion chamber, the turbine blades and the reheat assembly.

There are many criteria by which an aero-engine may be judged. Airline engineering staffs tend to use the yardsticks of reliability and ease of maintenance, and the Olympus designers had these objectives very much in mind from the outset. By the time Concorde enters airline service, its engines will have been more comprehensively tested than any other

Above: The Olympus 593 twin-spool turbojet, produced by the Bristol Engine Division of Rolls-Royce in Britain and SNECMA in France. The Olympus 593 has demonstrated a thrust of over 40,000 lb. – equal to the total brake-horsepower of 10,000 Minis. Reproduced from a drawing provided by Rolls-Royce (Bristol) Ltd. Right: The layout of the engine showing the different materials used; exhaustive metallurgical research was undertaken before deciding on the most suitable alloys. Left: A photograph showing the ease of access ensured by the mounting of the engines in paired nacelles beneath the wing. This positioning also minimises changes in intake flow direction during take-off and final approach.

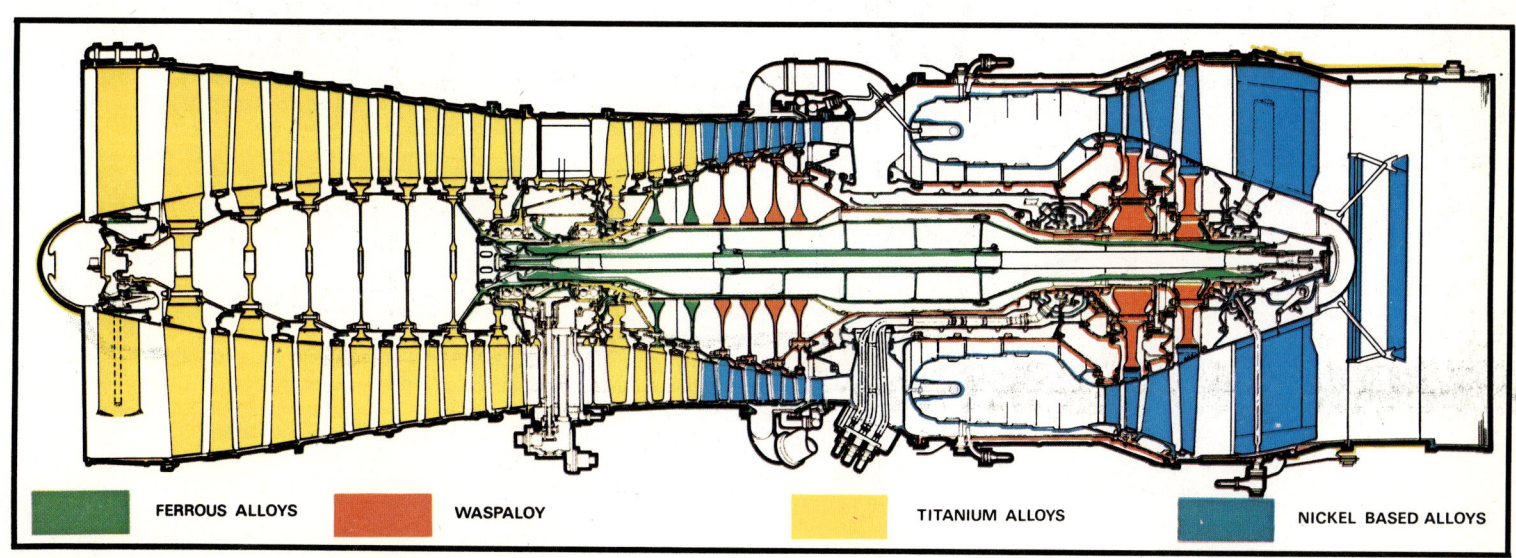

type and will be backed by the experience of 46,000 hours of operation on test-beds or in flight. The Olympus is also a modular design and can be broken down into 12 main assemblies to speed up overhaul procedures. Internal inspection of the engine can be made, without removing it from its nacelle, by *borescope*, an instrument first developed for use in aero-engine research and ground testing.

Air intake system
The engine air intake system is one of the most remarkable pieces of equipment in the Concorde, and its efficiency is of critical importance to the overall perform-

ance of the aircraft. Taking in air at speeds up to Mach 2.2, the intake has to deliver it in an even flow to the face of the engine at a speed of Mach 0.5. So, at supersonic cruise, there is a four-fold deceleration of the intake air from 1,350mph to about 350mph in the length of the intake, a distance of 11ft. Apart from that, the amount of air (the mass air flow) has to be precisely adjusted to the requirements of the engines which, as already explained, vary considerably over the speed range.

These necessary variations in mass air flow can be achieved only by altering the size of the intake throat; by making it, in the engineering term, a *variable geometry*

intake rather than a fixed one. In Concorde the variation of the intake geometry is obtained by the use of two movable ramps in the roof of the intake and a spill door in the intake floor. In the spill door there is a small flap that opens inwards to serve as an auxiliary air inlet when required. Automatic control of the movable ramps is effected through electronic black boxes. Pressure sensors in the intake provide continuous information from which the control unit is able to calculate the right position for the ramps and actuate the ramp mechanism accordingly.

At take-off and in climb the ramps are in the fully open position, the spill door is

| ■ FERROUS ALLOYS | ■ WASPALOY | ■ TITANIUM ALLOYS | ■ NICKEL BASED ALLOYS |

closed and its inlet flap is open (the intake configuration at landing is similar). As subsonic speed increases in the climb, the flap is gradually closed but the ramps remain open until the aircraft reaches a speed of about Mach 1.3 (nearly 1,000mph). As supersonic speed increases above that point, the ramps are automatically lowered and this sets up a series of controlled shock waves within the intake. These shock waves slow the intake air down to subsonic speed before it reaches the engine.

When Concorde's powerplant was designed, it was regarded as a daring innovation to propose the use of reheat on an engine for a civil aircraft. Up till that time, reheat systems had been used only on military aeroplanes. The reheat system is situated aft of the turbine and is used to provide additional thrust by igniting fuel in the jet pipe.

For a supersonic transport, one advantage of reheat is that it provides a considerable increase in take-off thrust without any great weight penalty. Reheat is also employed in transonic acceleration to reduce the total flight fuel consumption, for although the use of reheat during the acceleration phase increases the immediate fuel consumption, there is a benefit in getting faster to the supersonic cruise speed at which consumption is at its lowest.

Exhaust nozzles

In a supersonic aircraft, the exhaust system has to incorporate variable geometry features to provide the required variations in the exhaust gas stream. This is the one area of the Concorde powerplant that has undergone major redevelopment since the original design. Subsonic aircraft exhaust their turbojet gases through a *convergent* nozzle which, by forcing the gases to pass through a smaller orifice, increase the thrust they produce. Engine efficiency in a supersonic aircraft can be improved by installing a second *divergent* nozzle to permit expansion of the gases. A convergent-divergent exhaust nozzle system was an integral part of the Concorde powerplant design from the beginning, and its development to the present high level of efficiency is a considerable achievement.

One of the many problems has been to provide a divergent nozzle that allowed the required exhaust expansion without causing external drag in supersonic operation. Both the exhaust nozzles are variable-geometry features. Variations in the area of the primary nozzle are used to control the turbine temperatures and rpm while variations in the secondary nozzle area ensure the efficient expansion of the primary gas stream.

Concorde's wide speed range demands careful matching of the intake/exhaust systems to the engines. The diagram (left) shows the disposition of intake surfaces and exhaust nozzles during different operations. Above: The second prototype outside the Filton assembly hall during the ground tests which preceded its first flight.

The production-standard secondary exhaust nozzle, known as the TRA (for "Thrust Reverser Aft"), is notable as an area of Concorde in which American designers have made a direct contribution. In this nozzle the main components are two "buckets," shaped like clamshells, which open and close vertically across the jet streams from each pair of engines. To meet the severe operating conditions, the buckets are made of a special welded steel honeycomb material whose manufacturers, Stresskin Products Co. of California, worked closely with SNECMA and BAC engineers on the design of the TRA nozzle. At take-off the secondary nozzle is

RAMP DOORS   SECONDRY AIR DOORS   PRIMARY NOZZLE   SECONDARY NOZZLE BUCKETS

(A) TAKE-OFF

SPILL DOOR/ IN LET FLAP   ENGINE BAY VENTILATION DOOR   SPADE SILENCERS

(B) NOISE ABATEMENT CLIMB

SHOCK PATTERN

(C) SUPERSONIC CRUISE

(D) ENGINE SHUT-DOWN

(E) REVERSE THRUST   AIRFLOW

partially closed, and during this phase the movement of the exhaust buckets, in conjunction with operation of the silencers, reduces the take-off noise levels. During the transonic acceleration, the buckets are moved progressively to the fully open position which they maintain throughout supersonic cruise. For reverse thrust, the buckets are closed across the gas stream, thus deflecting it in a forward direction upwards and downwards.

Deciding on a maximum speed

In any supersonic transport design, the most critical decision is the choice of cruise speed, for this has a profound bearing on the aircraft's aerodynamic configuration, its structure and the type of material used. Working independently, French and British engineers had opted for a Mach 2.2 (1,400mph) cruise speed. Later in the Concorde project this was slightly reduced, for structural life reasons, to Mach 2 (1,350mph). There are two basic reasons why the French and British – and the Russians – thought that Mach 2.2 or

thereabouts was the right speed for supersonic air travel. One, variation of structure temperatures with speed; and two, overall efficiency.

Supersonic aircraft fly slower than sound as well as faster than sound. Therefore the Concorde structure and all its systems had to be designed to function efficiently over a much wider temperature range than those of any previous airliner. They had to cope with temperatures as low as $-45°C$, encountered flying at subsonic speeds in the icy upper atmosphere, to $+150°C$, encountered in supersonic flight, for the temperature of an aircraft structure rises rapidly as the cruise speed increases.

At Mach 1 (750mph) the average temperature of the structure is still just below $0°C$, but at Mach 2 it has risen to about $120°C$, higher than the boiling point of water. By the time a cruise speed of Mach 3 (2,000mph) is reached, the structure temperature has risen to about $300°C$, approaching the melting point of lead and well above that of tin!

Materials testing was already under way

in both countries, and the indications were that the upper temperature limit that could be accepted for an aluminium structure was around Mach 2.2. To go for anything much faster than that would mean designing the structure in a stainless steel or titanium alloy. This would have meant a much longer development period and greatly increased development costs.

By that time, aircraft designers and production engineers had been specifying and using aluminium alloys for over 40 years and were thoroughly familiar with its virtues and its limitations. That was one powerful motive for the decision to build the SST in aluminium. Another was the minimal time advantage that a Mach 3 airliner would show over a Mach 2.2 type. A Mach 2.2 airliner would halve the subsonic flight time across the North Atlantic from seven hours to three and a half hours, but the Mach 3 airliner would cut only an additional 20 minutes of the Mach 2.2 time.

Two factors had to be taken into account in assessing overall efficiency – aerodynamic efficiency and propulsive efficiency.

Aerodynamic efficiency is at its best at a speed of Mach 0.80 (600mph). As speed rises to Mach 1 (750mph) there is a sudden falling off. The sharp decline continues until about Mach 1.4 (1,050mph), and, between Mach 1.4 and Mach 3 (2,000mph), although there is still a decline, it is much more gradual.

This decline in aerodynamic efficiency is offset, however, by the propulsive efficiency "curve" of the turbojet engine, which rises steadily to Mach 3 and a little beyond. (It should be made clear at this point that we are speaking of the straight turbojet: the efficiency of the high bypass-ratio engine – the *fanjet* used in modern wide-bodied subsonic airliners – starts to decline just before the speed of sound is reached).

The result of offsetting the loss of aerodynamic efficiency against the increased propulsive efficiency of the turbojet as speed increases, is that overall efficiency

The choice of a cruising speed of Mach 2.2 was determined by a variety of factors. Once the basic configuration of the aircraft was decided, extensive testing of the basic shape had to be carried out in hydrodynamic tunnels (above) and wind tunnels.

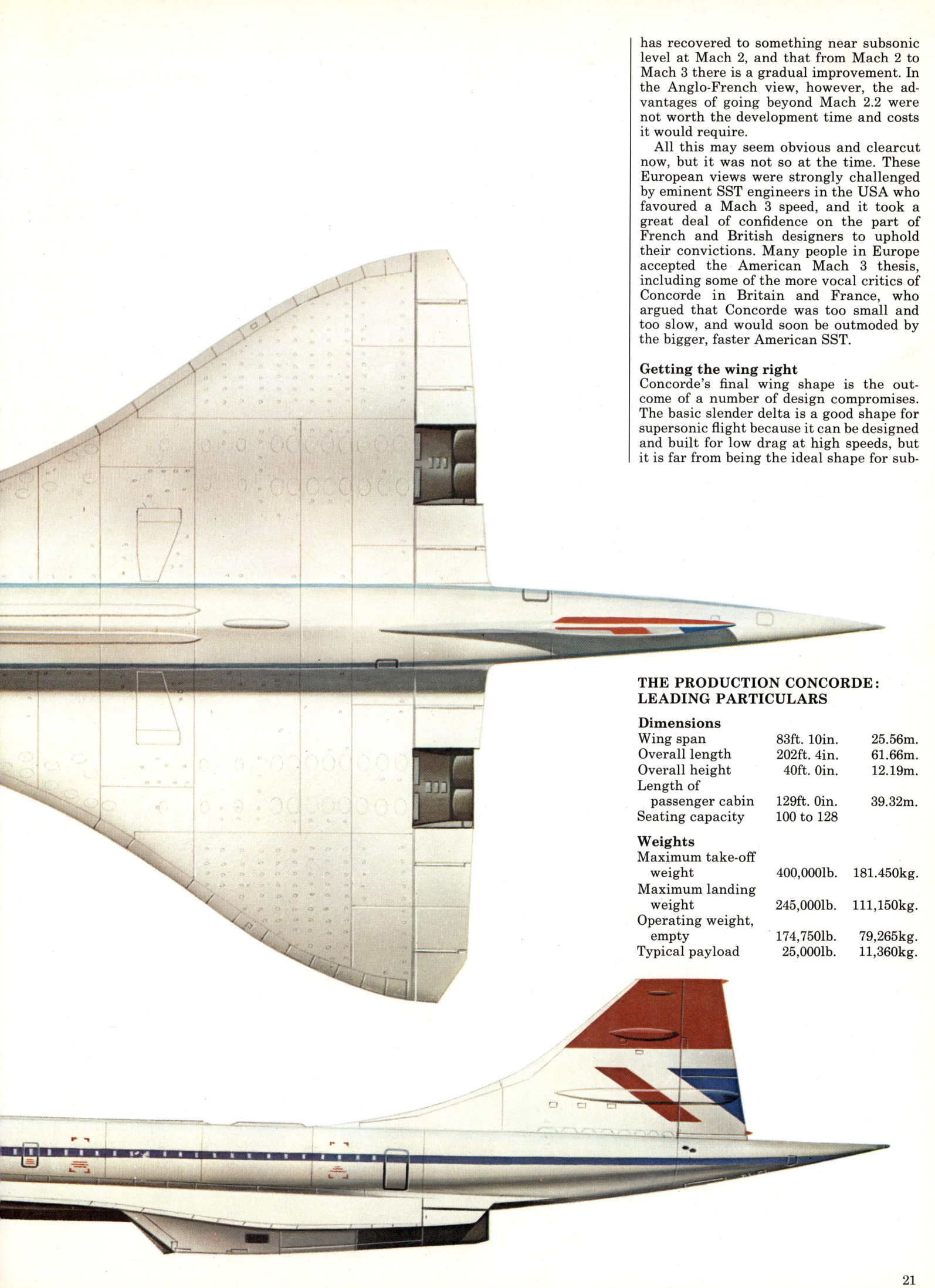

has recovered to something near subsonic level at Mach 2, and that from Mach 2 to Mach 3 there is a gradual improvement. In the Anglo-French view, however, the advantages of going beyond Mach 2.2 were not worth the development time and costs it would require.

All this may seem obvious and clearcut now, but it was not so at the time. These European views were strongly challenged by eminent SST engineers in the USA who favoured a Mach 3 speed, and it took a great deal of confidence on the part of French and British designers to uphold their convictions. Many people in Europe accepted the American Mach 3 thesis, including some of the more vocal critics of Concorde in Britain and France, who argued that Concorde was too small and too slow, and would soon be outmoded by the bigger, faster American SST.

Getting the wing right

Concorde's final wing shape is the outcome of a number of design compromises. The basic slender delta is a good shape for supersonic flight because it can be designed and built for low drag at high speeds, but it is far from being the ideal shape for sub-

THE PRODUCTION CONCORDE: LEADING PARTICULARS

Dimensions

Wing span	83ft. 10in.	25.56m.
Overall length	202ft. 4in.	61.66m.
Overall height	40ft. 0in.	12.19m.
Length of passenger cabin	129ft. 0in.	39.32m.
Seating capacity	100 to 128	

Weights

Maximum take-off weight	400,000lb.	181.450kg.
Maximum landing weight	245,000lb.	111,150kg.
Operating weight, empty	174,750lb.	79,265kg.
Typical payload	25,000lb.	11,360kg.

sonic speeds. Good control and handling qualities have to be "designed into" the slender delta.

In the Concorde design, the option of using a variable-geometry wing – a swing wing – in order to get the best of both supersonic and subsonic worlds had been firmly rejected on grounds of weight and complexity. It took a continuing programme of research and development extending over a number of years to evolve the final wing shape. This was necessarily a lengthy process because all the successive changes had to be exhaustively tested, first in the wind-tunnels and then in the air. Increases in wing area and subtle reshaping of the wing tips and leading edges have made for better low-speed controllability and an improved lift-drag ratio at subsonic speeds.

Wing-design was another factor favouring the adoption at Mach 2.2 as the upper limit for the cruise speed. At that speed the designer can achieve a good working compromise between conflicting supersonic and

Concorde in the livery of British Airways photographed in the course of a test flight from its United Kingdom base at Fairford in Gloucestershire.

Concorde in the colours of Air France.

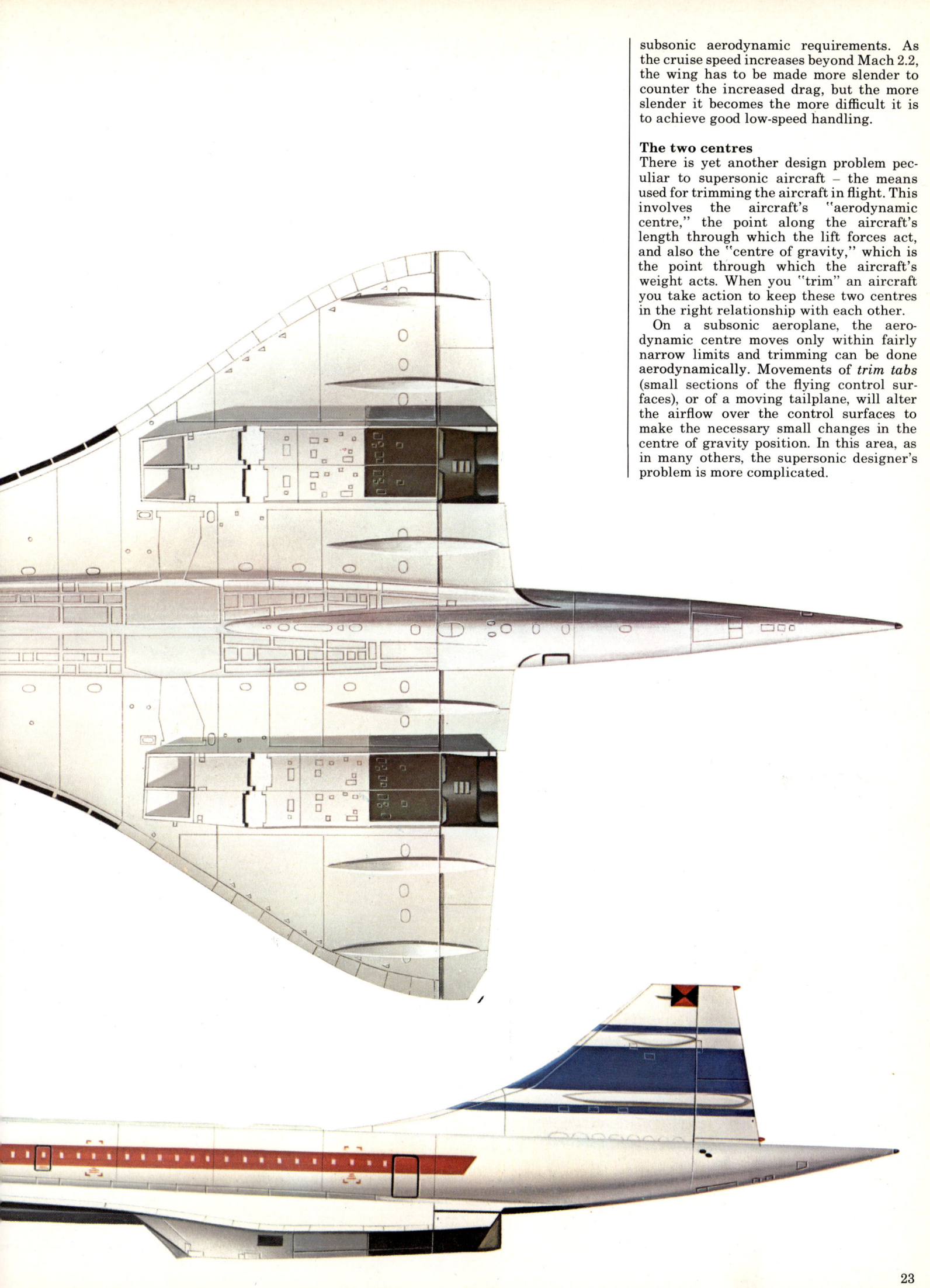

subsonic aerodynamic requirements. As the cruise speed increases beyond Mach 2.2, the wing has to be made more slender to counter the increased drag, but the more slender it becomes the more difficult it is to achieve good low-speed handling.

The two centres
There is yet another design problem peculiar to supersonic aircraft – the means used for trimming the aircraft in flight. This involves the aircraft's "aerodynamic centre," the point along the aircraft's length through which the lift forces act, and also the "centre of gravity," which is the point through which the aircraft's weight acts. When you "trim" an aircraft you take action to keep these two centres in the right relationship with each other.

On a subsonic aeroplane, the aerodynamic centre moves only within fairly narrow limits and trimming can be done aerodynamically. Movements of *trim tabs* (small sections of the flying control surfaces), or of a moving tailplane, will alter the airflow over the control surfaces to make the necessary small changes in the centre of gravity position. In this area, as in many others, the supersonic designer's problem is more complicated.

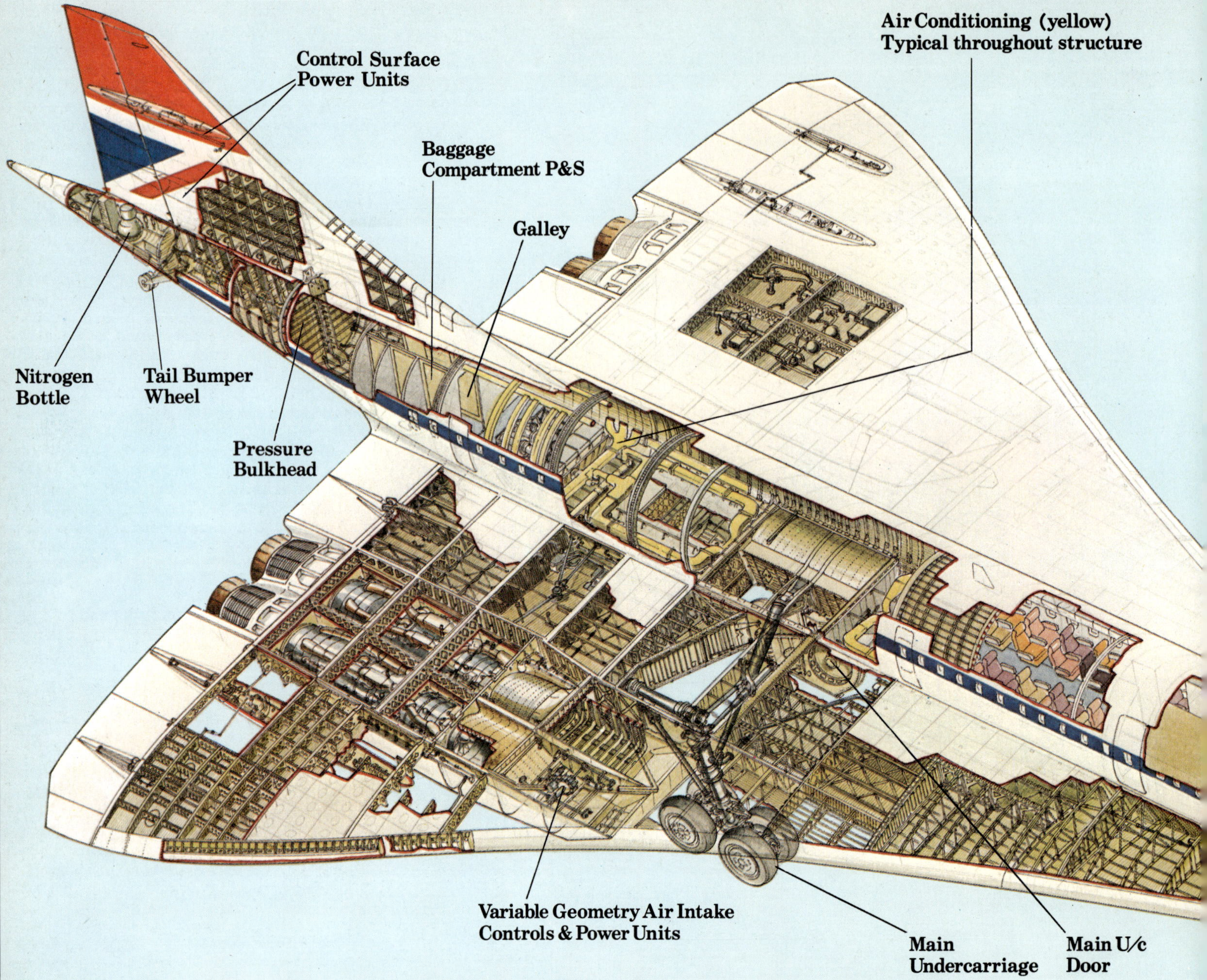

Control Surface Power Units

Air Conditioning (yellow) Typical throughout structure

Baggage Compartment P&S

Galley

Nitrogen Bottle

Tail Bumper Wheel

Pressure Bulkhead

Variable Geometry Air Intake Controls & Power Units

Main Undercarriage

Main U/c Door

FUEL TRANSFER MOVEMENTS

Concorde's fuel management system plays a vital role in controlling and adjusting the aircraft's centre of gravity to match the differing needs of subsonic and supersonic flight. During acceleration to supersonic speed, fuel is transferred rearward from the front trim tanks; during deceleration to subsonic speed, the opposite process takes place, with fuel being moved forward from the rear trim tank. Trimming by the aerodynamic methods employed on subsonic aircraft is ruled out in supersonic flight because of the unacceptable level of drag which would be caused.

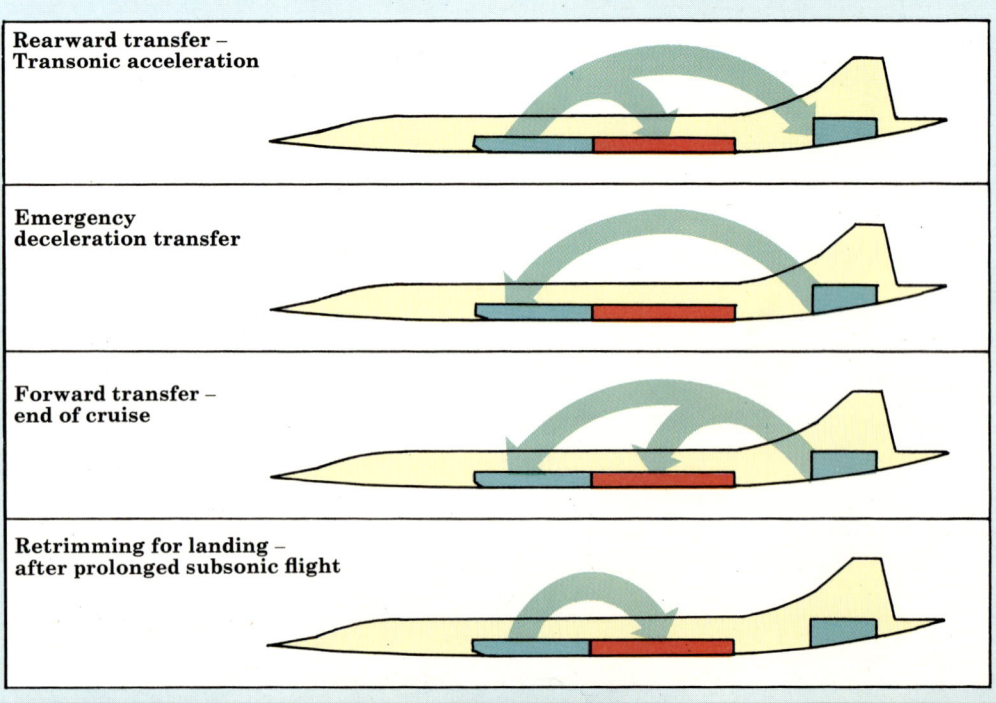

Rearward transfer – Transonic acceleration

Emergency deceleration transfer

Forward transfer – end of cruise

Retrimming for landing – after prolonged subsonic flight

■ Main tanks   ■ Trim tanks

When a supersonic aircraft accelerates from subsonic speed up through the transonic range to supersonic speed, its aerodynamic centre moves aft. In Concorde, the cambering of the wing and the "wine-glass" line of the leading edge both help to reduce this movement, but it is still appreciable. If no action were taken to change the centre of gravity, the result of moving the centre of lift towards the rear would be to raise the tail end of the aircraft and so put it into a nose-down attitude, resulting in greater drag and more difficult control.

To make the adjustment by aerodynamic methods as in the subsonic aircraft is not feasible because any deflection of flying control surfaces would have to be made throughout the supersonic cruise and would cause unacceptable drag. In Concorde the method used to keep the centre of gravity in the right place is to pump fuel between the main tanks and forward and aft trim tanks as required.

It is true that the supersonic designer is beset with new problems, but the airflow characteristics of the slender delta give him at least one natural advantage over the subsonic designer. Nature has provided the delta wing with its own "high lift device" and there is no need for the complicated arrangement of slots and flaps that can be

Clearly seen, half-raised, in this photograph is the visor which protects the flight deck windows in high-speed flight. The need to cope with an unprecedentedly wide range of temperatures necessitated a speed-up of development of glass technology and resulted in advances in the design of high-strength glass.

seen on a subsonic wing when the aircraft takes off or comes in to land.

To make its landing approach at a safe speed, a delta aircraft assumes a fairly steep angle of attack. At take-off it is also at a steeper angle than a subsonic type. At these high angles of incidence, the airflow over the leading edge of the wing breaks away and forms a vortex. If this vortex formation remains stable (and the Concorde leading edge is designed to keep it stable) it follows the line of the leading

edge and, has the effect of producing additional lift in just those two phases of flight – landing and take-off – when the subsonic aircraft has to use mechanical means to get added lift.

The droop snoot
Besides the powerplant and fuel system, the Concorde's adjustable droop nose is another design feature that differs markedly from subsonic practice. A movable nose is required on a supersonic airliner to give the pilots a good view of the airport runway in landing and take-off. The nose of a supersonic transport, unlike the blunt rounded front end of the subsonic airliner, is streamlined for high speeds. It is long and tapers to a sharp point. Concorde comes in to land and takes off at a more nose-up attitude than a subsonic aircraft, and, if it were fixed, the long nose could hamper the view from the flight deck on to the runway.

To get over this problem, the nose unit (all that part of the fuselage forward of the flight deck) is made so that it can be lowered during landing and take-off and raised during the other phases of the flight. The droop nose is composed of two sections: the main nose structure and the glazed upper section of the forward fuselage, known as the visor, which can be lowered and raised independently.

In supersonic cruise, the nose and the visor are raised. This streamlines the front end of the aircraft to minimise air resistance, and the visor protects the flight deck windows against kinetic heating and air pressure. Forward view from the flight deck is through the flight windows and the visor windows. At take-off and in the early stage of the subsonic climb, the visor is lowered and the nose is lowered to its intermediate position, 5° of droop. In subsonic cruise the visor is lowered but the nose is raised. In the approach, and at landing, and also while taxying at the airport, the visor is lowered and the nose is in the down position, 12½° of droop.

With the droop nose, which has been thoroughly tested in the most extreme climatic conditions, the Concorde pilot's view on to the runway is better than that from the flight deck of most other airliners.

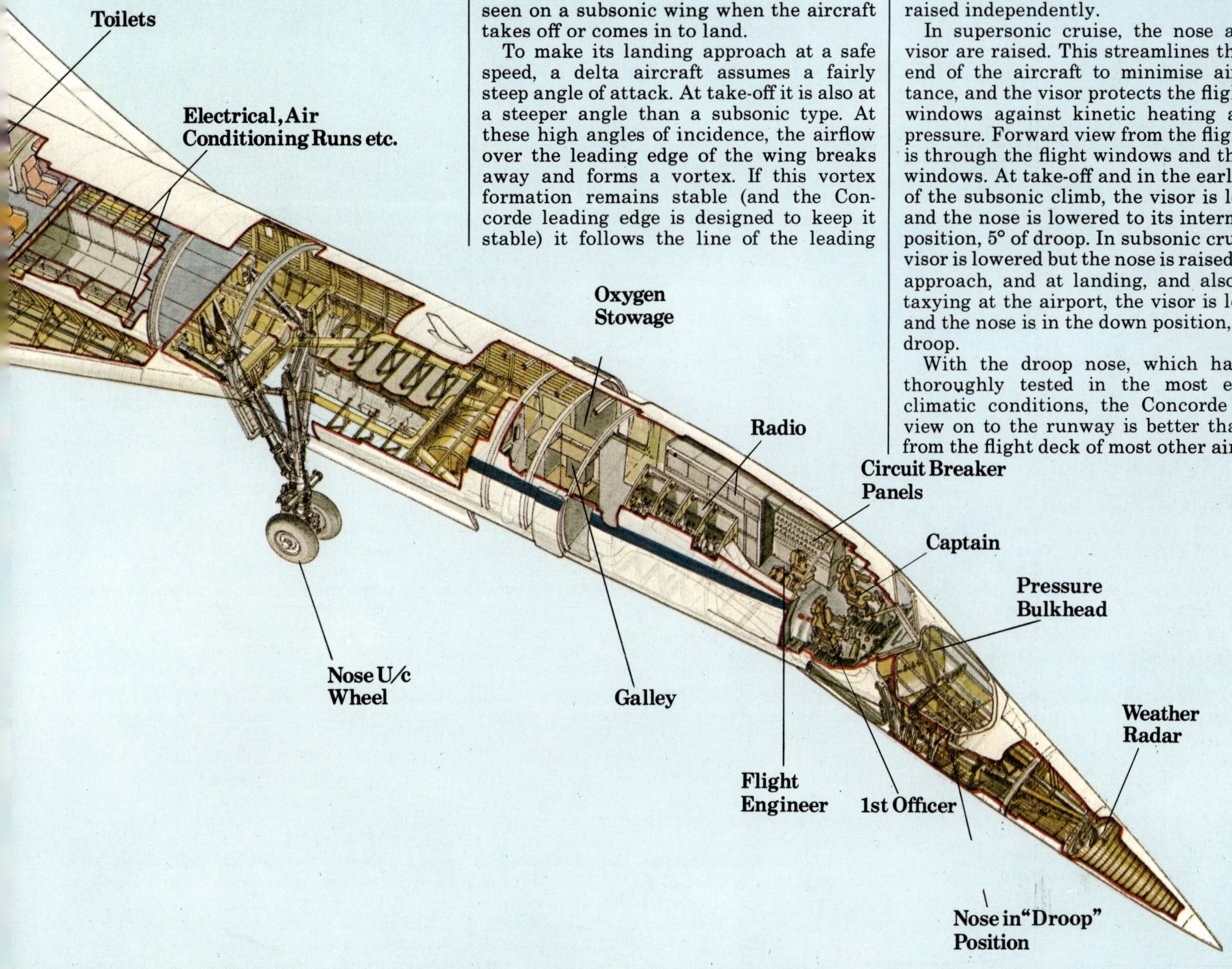

Toilets

Electrical, Air Conditioning Runs etc.

Oxygen Stowage

Radio

Circuit Breaker Panels

Captain

Pressure Bulkhead

Nose U/c Wheel

Galley

Weather Radar

Flight Engineer

1st Officer

Nose in "Droop" Position

GETTING AIRBORNE

There are no ivory towers for the designer of commercial aircraft for the simple reason that his product has to be what that term for it implies: a commercial proposition. He cannot work successfully in isolation from market considerations. The joint proposal for a supersonic airliner put forward by Sud-Aviation and BAC was a merging of the two separate approaches to the problem: the French medium-range approach and the British long-range approach. Within the same overall dimensions, the joint design team was offering a 100-seat medium-range vehicle and a heavier 90-seat long-range vehicle.

Selling an idea

An input was also needed from the market. What was the reaction of the potential customers among the airlines to the preliminary proposals? Before the designers went too far down the road with their own ideas, they must discover what the operators were thinking. So, in the early months of 1963, the sales teams were out on the road making their first presentations of Concorde to major airlines. These were Anglo-French teams, and there has been close integration of the marketing effort ever since those early days. If the airline being visited was one with which Sud-Aviation had had the closer contact in the past, then a Frenchman led the presentation team; if the visit was to a BAC contact, a Briton led.

The reception given to the marketing teams by the airlines was generally friendly, but could not, by any stretch of the imagination, have been described as enthusiastic. This was hardly to be wondered at since many of them were either facing, or expec-ting to face, problems of over-capacity caused by the introduction of the new generation of subsonic jetliners. With too many seats chasing too few passengers, the operators could hardly be expected to welcome the prospect of a new type of airliner making their equipment obsolescent.

Apart from this, there were several specific criticisms of the preliminary proposals. There was a general acceptance of the Anglo-French design philosophy of a Mach 2.2 aluminium alloy airliner, but there were reservations about payload and about the fuel reserve allowances that the designers had made in their estimates.

The 90-seat payload proposed for the long-range aircraft was thought to be too small to enable an economic operation to be carried on. More capacity was essential in the airline view, despite the makers' arguments that the high speed of Concorde would give it the productivity of a subsonic aircraft twice its size (because, in a given time, Concorde could produce twice the number of "seat-miles" produced by the subsonic type).

Fuel reserve policies vary considerably from airline to airline. Normally when an aircraft manufacturer makes a presentation of a new type to a potential customer he will know that customer's policy on reserves, and will use this figure in making his forecasts of how his aircraft will perform in the airline's service.

Concorde's manufacturers had felt, with the support of some national aviation authorities such as the USA's Federal Aviation Administration, that fuel reserve allowances for a supersonic airliner should not necessarily be the same as those for a subsonic airliner. There were sound reasons for this view, notably the fact that, at the much higher cruise altitudes, atmospheric conditions are calmer, there is less wind and consequently fuel requirements can be more precisely calculated in advance. These and other arguments have come to be more generally accepted in recent years and new supersonic fuel reserve policies are being formulated, but in 1963 any suggestion of lower fuel reserves was firmly rejected.

An even more important reaction from this first round of talks with the airlines was that any customer interest in a supersonic airliner was centred on the long-range proposal. The marketing teams reported that, for the time being, it would be necessary to concentrate the joint design effort on modifying and developing the long-range version to get it closer to the airline requirement. With some understandable reluctance on the part of the French, design work on the medium-range version was discontinued and has never since been revived.

Thus the verdict of the market had gone in favour of the British view that the first-generation SST must be a design with Transatlantic range. This point is not made here in a spirit of nationalism. The French arguments for the medium-range version had much force and logic behind them, and it will be recalled that the British Supersonic Transport Aircraft Committee had itself put forward proposals for both a long-range and a medium-range SST. The real significance of this decision, taken so early in the project, was that it was made in response to market opinion.

The general impression gained by the sales teams was that they had been told by the operators: "Back to the drawing board, my friends, and come and see us again when you have done a whole lot more work on

this supersonic aeroplane of yours." Despite this, in June, 1963 Pan American took an option on six Concordes followed by Continental Airlines (three) in July, American Airlines (four) in October and TWA (four) in November. It was also agreed that the first 18 Concordes should be delivered on rotation, six to Pan Am, six to BOAC (as it then was) and six to Air France.

The threat of U.S. competition

If the Pan American motive had partly been to inject more urgency into the American SST project, it had the desired effect. Within a day or so President Kennedy proclaimed his government's intention to support the American aircraft industry in developing and building a supersonic transport that would be bigger and faster than the Concorde. An options list was opened and many of the world's leading airlines, including all those on the Concorde option list, put their names down for the American aircraft. The aim was to get it into service within two or three years after Concorde, and, in view of the American industry's great reputation for getting things done on time, this announcement caused some concern in Britain and France.

This concern was not fully shared by the Anglo-French design team. If the Americans really were going for a Mach 3 (or even, as it later became, a Mach 2.7) SST built in titanium, the Concorde men were convinced that, even with the USA's immense resources and enormous drive, it would take at least a decade to get their aircraft into service. To carry the 75,000lb. payload being spoken of would mean a take-off weight of not less than one million pounds. The aircraft would be at least 300 feet long

Advancing mirage – photo-sequence of take-off run during tests at Casablanca.

(the length of a football field), and the structural problems of building an airframe of that length in titanium were mind-boggling. At the very least, Concorde would have a five-year lead over the American aircraft.

What really concerned the Concorde's makers, in 1963 and later when the American SST was cancelled, was that the Americans might change their minds about cruise speed and elect to build a Mach 2.2 airliner. This would have been a much more worrying prospect.

In their predictions about the American SST problems, the Concorde designers were right. In their predictions about their own entry into service date, they were years out. The design problems that lay ahead for them might not be of the same magnitude as those which brought the American SST to a halt, but they were still sufficiently formidable to throw an optimistic timetable well out of gear. To get the required greater passenger carrying capacity in the long-range version meant carrying more fuel and that meant increased take-off weight and that, in turn, meant more engine power. It is a familiar story in aviation, and especially to the engine manufacturer, who sometimes feels that he is "tail-end Charlie" in this situation.

Meeting the client's needs

However, like all good engine designs the Olympus 593 had development, or "stretch," potential, and the engine manufacturers were able to offer an increase in power sufficient to meet the first aircraft growth

stage. This stage took the all-up weight from the 262,000lb. of the preliminary design up to 286,000lb. and the seating capacity from 90 to 100. The first airline response to this increase was not encouraging; it was regarded as no more than a step in the right direction.

Further progress depended on greater engine power, and Bristol Siddeley and SNECMA decided on a redesign of the Olympus to provide a reserve, not only for the immediate situation but for the future weight increases that would occur in Concorde development as they do in every other civil aircraft programme. The new engine was given the designation 593B.

With the assurance of additional power, the redesign of the aircraft could go forward. An increase was made in the wing and fin area, additional underfloor fuel tankage was provided and, to compensate for the loss of baggage space that this caused, extra space for baggage stowage was provided in the rear fuselage. This was made available by eliminating the ventral passenger door originally proposed and substituting for it a second port-side door.

These changes had the effect of increasing the maximum take-off weight to 326,000lb. and the passenger capacity to 118. Although development went on for much of 1964, this design was essentially the Concorde prototype design. Early in 1965 it was "frozen" (which meant that no major changes were to be subsequently introduced) and the first metal was cut for the two prototype aircraft.

By then BOAC, Air France and Pan American had each increased their options from six to eight; Middle East Airlines and Qantas had joined the options list; and the

total number of options had risen to 43. In the short space of twelve months there had been an astonishing transformation in the market prospects for Concorde.

This account of Concorde development has so far been mainly concerned with the policy makers, and the designers and the marketing men. It is now time to give some attention to the production men; the engineers, the planners, the progress chasers, the foremen and charge-hands, the machinists and the fitters – all those people who sometimes lump themselves together under the mock-modest title of "tinbashers."

Building the first Concordes was, by any standard, a formidable engineering task. More than 100,000 detail drawings were issued to the production organisation. The parts list for the aircraft finally contained more than a quarter of a million items, and a "part number" could refer to a single small bolt or to a large bought-out compo-

nent like a generator (which would itself be made up of hundreds of separate parts). Nobody ever had the time to work out just how many separate parts went into the building of a Concorde prototype, but the total certainly exceeded one million.

It would be quite wrong to give the impression that in the two years, 1963 and 1964, when the design was moving forward from the preliminary to the prototype stage, the production engineers were held up for work. The agreement on the manufacturing breakdown, to which they had contributed, enabled them to begin their planning in earnest.

There were shops to be laid out and men to be trained, new machine tools to be ordered and transport requirements to be worked out. Above all, there was the essential job, for the top production men, of "getting to know the French" (or the English). Initially, most of the Anglo-

Above, left and right: Interior and exterior views of the first Concorde prototype, 001, being assembled at the Aérospatiale factory at Toulouse.

The Concorde programme stimulated the development of a number of advanced manufacturing processes and production techniques with the object of saving weight and costs and improving product quality. Right: Laser beam welding, which is being developed for more accurate welding even than electron beam welding. BAC Filton now has one of Europe's largest electron beam chambers. Far right: The highly sophisticated tape-controlled machining operations, which can produce a component to closer tolerances than are possible by traditional methods.

French contacts had been at the design level. Now, the manufacturing men had to talk together to discover how best they could work together. In this field, too, French and British engineers have proved that they make a most effective partnership, founded on mutual respect and on a common faith in the project.

While the production planning was going on, machine and assembly shops were gaining experience in handling the new (to them) RR58 aluminium alloy by building test specimens. These were small assemblies at first, but gradually increased in size until major components were being produced for the laboratories. As had been expected, the new material presented no serious problems for the machine shops; it could be handled and fabricated using techniques that were already tested and proved, which was one of the reasons why it had been selected.

Sculpture milling

One of those techniques is the process known as *sculpture milling* or machining *from the solid*, using tape-controlled machine tools. In this process, the modern production engineer has gone back to the principles of the primitive dug-out canoe. Instead of "building up" a structural component by welding or riveting, he starts with a solid billet of metal and uses a milling machine to carve the required shape out of it.

For Concorde, the process offered two important advantages: structural integrity and weight-saving. The technique is sometimes known as *integral* milling and it was the promise it held out of increased strength that first attracted the interest of production engineers. Any joint or weld is a source of possible weakness, and an assembly that has no joints or welds will be potentially that much the stronger. So the process is well suited for producing Concorde components that are highly stressed, like the wing or fin, or in which there are "cut-outs", like the window panels.

Weight-saving, the second advantage, is entirely due to the fact that, correctly programmed, the tape-controlled machine tool can produce a component to closer tolerances than are possible by traditional methods. On the Concorde structure as a whole, savings which amount to some hundreds of pounds have been made in this way. A saving of "some hundreds of pounds" may not sound impressive, but structure weight is a critical factor in the design of an economic supersonic transport. Every additional pound of structure weight in the Concorde requires about an additional pound of fuel to carry it across the Atlantic, and that extra pound of fuel will, in turn, need a second pound of fuel to carry *it*. Every pound of structure that can be saved, therefore, means a saving of three pounds in take-off weight – which explains why Concorde designers are more weight-conscious than the most ardent slimmer.

The double "learning curve"

In the past, the Concorde manufacturing organisation, and in particular the provision of two separate final assembly lines, one at Filton and the other at Toulouse, has been the subject of adverse comment. Duplication of assembly lines could not be avoided in 1962 however, because it would not have been politically acceptable to have all Concordes assembled in one country. Most outside criticism is not, however,

directed at the right target – which is the duplication of the "learning curve", a term that needs a little explanation.

When series production of a new engineering product is begun, everyone concerned has to "learn" how to do his new job. There will be machines to set up, new machining processes to be mastered, jobs to be timed and rates to be fixed. Machinists, fitters, inspectors, supervisors will be feeling their way, and the whole exercise has to be carefully "run in" like a new car.

All this takes time, and, on the production line, time spells money. The first new products off the line, whether they be aeroplanes or washing machines, will cost much more to produce than the price at which they will be sold. That price is based on the assumption that as the workpeople get into the swing of the new job, output will improve and the cost curve will come down steadily until it levels out below the price line. That first downward movement of the curve is called the "learning curve."

If there are two assembly lines with two lots of people doing the same job, there are obviously going to be two learning curves. To offset the effect of this, BAC and Aérospatiale have made a new approach to aircraft assembly. Up to now, airframe components have been put together on the final assembly jig to form a shell structure, and then all the aircraft systems have been laboriously installed in the shell. In Concorde assembly, much of the work of installing systems is done at the component build stage and the components come, fully equipped, to the final assembly line. This cuts down the work of final assembly and moves much of the learning curve out to the sub-assembly where there is no duplication.

One example of such a fully-equipped component is the nose and forward fuselage built at Weybridge, a 50ft.-long section comprising the flight deck, the forward part of the passenger cabin and the nose landing gear bay. When this component is delivered to the final assembly lines, it is equipped with its cabin insulation and the relevant segments of the electrical, hydraulic, flying control and air-conditioning systems, incorporating 25,000 parts and 90 miles of wiring.

Although the basic structural material used in Concorde is an aluminium alloy, titanium and stainless steel are employed in local areas of high stress and high

Right: Concordes in production in the huge assembly hall at BAC's Filton factory. Below: Electricians installing wiring in the flight deck.

temperature such as the engine bays. Valuable experience has been gained in working with these metals of the future, and advanced manufacturing methods have been developed for dealing with the special problems they present.

In aircraft production welding of titanium has proved extremely difficult in the past because the welding heat source, or beam, has to be directed with pinpoint accuracy on to the weld if the strength characteristics of the surrounding metal are not to be adversely affected. Electron beam welding provides this standard of accuracy, and BAC Filton now has one of Europe's largest electron beam welding chambers. Titanium components can now be satisfactorily built up by welding, allowing smaller billets to be used and thus saving considerable production cost.

Even more advanced laser beam processes are under development. At Filton a special department is engaged on testing and developing advanced manufacturing processes with the object of saving weight and cost and improving product quality. New methods of producing intricate component shapes, such as explosive forming and chemical etching, have been adopted and adapted to the special needs of Concorde.

Aeronautical engineering is acknowledged to be the spearhead of advanced technology. The challenge of measuring up to the new demands of a project like Concorde is a spur to progress in associated industries. New manufacturing methods and new machine tools are part of the response to the Concorde challenge.

Government fears

The Concorde development history can be regarded as falling into three phases: one, from the preliminary design stage in 1961–62 to the cutting of the first metal for the prototypes in April, 1965; two, from April, 1965 to the first flight of 01, the first pre-production aircraft in December, 1971; and three, from December, 1971 to entry into airline service around the end of 1975.

The second phase – getting the plane into the air – began in a general atmosphere of uncertainty and, in some quarters, of gloom and despondency, in sharp contrast to the euphoria felt a few months earlier. At some levels on the project, there were strained relations between British and French, in the aftermath of the crisis of confidence caused by the "review" of the project made by the Labour government when it took office in October, 1964.

They had announced that they wanted urgently to examine, with the French government, the development programme for Concorde. The French government agreed, but made it clear they were not prepared to countenance any suggestion that Concorde should be cancelled. The November, 1962 treaty contained no termination clause. Either directly or indirectly, the French let it be known that any unilateral decision to cancel by the British would be contested in the International Court of Justice at the Hague. In February, 1965 the British government announced that they intended to continue with the project in accordance with the terms of the 1962 treaty.

Those four months of uncertainty, however, had a traumatic effect on morale in BAC factories engaged on Concorde design and production. Work went on and there were close contacts with the French at working level, but there was an air of unreality about the daily activities. When the decision to proceed was announced, there was relief but also a sense that government support was something less than whole-hearted. Many people working on the project were left with the impression that the final fate of Concorde was likely to depend as much on politics as on its design and performance.

At this time it was accepted that the prototype design, now frozen for manufacture, was an interim design; it was not going to provide the payload-range capability that airlines demanded. Nevertheless, work went ahead because this was an utterly new breed of commercial aircraft and getting a plane into the air and gradually exploring the flight envelope was the only real way to know that the design worked. Maybe the production standard Concorde, when it emerged, would be different from the prototype, but the prototype would establish whether the basic design was right.

Meantime, the dialogue between the makers and the airlines continued, and always the pressure from the operators was for more payload. The design presented to the IATA technical committee in May, 1964 had been a 118-seater. A year later airlines were informed that a modified design was now being offered, with a seating capacity of 139 seats at a 34in. seating pitch and a take-off weight of 340,000lb. This became known as the "pre-production" aircraft.

To obtain this 18 per cent increase in seating accommodation, the fuselage had been lengthened by about 6ft. 6in. and the rear pressure bulkhead had been moved aft 15ft. 8in., so increasing the length of the pressurised cabin by 19ft. 3in. The rear ventral door of the prototypes was replaced by two lateral doors at the rear of the cabin, the left side door being for passenger access and the right side door for ground servicing access. A total volumetric payload of 28,000lb. was offered, compared with the 23,600lb. of the prototype.

There was no increase in wing area from the prototype standard, but the results of the intensive aerodynamic research that had been going on showed themselves in

Opposite: Passengers in Concorde 02, one of the two pre-production aircraft, photographed while flying at over twice the speed of sound above the North Atlantic between Boston and Paris. Below: Diagram showing the passenger cabin in cross-section, with the main dimensions.

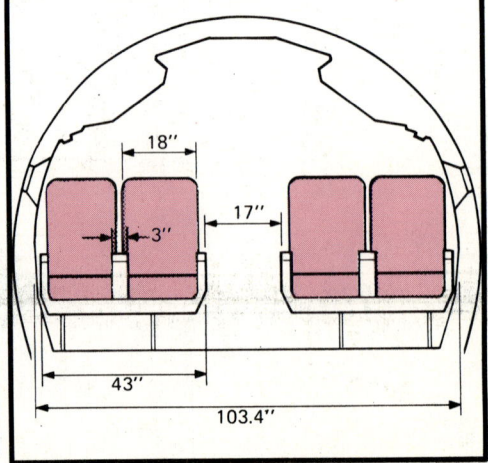

subtle re-shaping of the wing tip areas and other refinements. These changes gave the pre-production aircraft's improved performance and operating economics.

Airline reaction to this larger aircraft was much more favourable. Over the next two years a number of new airline names were added to the Concorde options list: Japan Air Lines (three aircraft), Sabena (two), Eastern Airlines (six), Braniff (three), United Airlines (six), Air Canada (four), Lufthansa (three). By mid-1967, 16 airlines had taken a total of 74 Concorde options.

The American SST

All these airlines had also taken options on the American SST, as had many other operators including the British and French flag carriers, BOAC and Air France. The American options total were nearly twice as large as Concorde's, and the list included the names of several prominent operators who had not taken Concorde options.

This point did not go unnoticed. Even among those who were well-disposed towards Concorde, fears were expressed that once again the pioneering would be done on one side of the Atlantic and the exploitation on the other. Those of this school of thought conceded that Concorde would be first into service but they asked: "Won't it soon be overtaken by the larger and faster American type? Isn't this the reasoning that has decided some very experienced operators to ignore Concorde and wait for the 2707?"

There was a recent precedent – the Comet and the 707 – that gave some weight to these views, but the two situations were very different. Concorde would have a substantial lead over the American aircraft in getting into service and at the worst (from the European viewpoint) this lead would be four or five years. That was too long a time for any major airline to stay uncompetitive by keeping out of supersonic operation. Unlike the Comet, Concorde would have a non-stop Transatlantic capability and would carry an economic payload. Most important of all, the productivity of the two SSTs would be so different that, when both were in service, they would each fit into a niche that the other could not fill.

Concorde would have four or five years to prove its time-saving attractions and its profitability – and to make the business traveller "supersonic-minded." When the 2707 entered service on the crack routes, Concorde would be operated on the many less densely-trafficked, but still important, routes on which the larger American aircraft would not be viable. There would be a place and a need for the two types as far ahead as one could see.

In the interval, the options arrangements had one great and lasting benefit for the Concorde manufacturers. Option-holding airlines seized the opportunity to take an active part in shaping the design. First into the field were the original three option-holders, Pan American, BOAC and Air France. They set up a technical committee – speedily nicknamed the "Troika" – to maintain liaison with the builders. All 16 American option-holders also formed a committee under the chairmanship of William Mentzer, president of United Airlines.

This was something without precedent in the civil aircraft business. Previously it had not been unusual for one or two major airlines to be associated with the development of an air transport design, and indeed the sales of some new types had been hampered

In March, 1969, Concorde began the most extensive flight test programme ever carried out by an airliner. The prototype is seen (left) ready for the ceremonial roll-out at Toulouse in December, 1967 and (right) taking off for the first time on March 2, 1969. It just missed being the world's first supersonic airliner to take to the air – the Soviet Tu 144 had flown on December 31, 1968.

Far right are seen three of the project's leaders: Brian Trubshaw, Director of Flight Test of BAC's Commercial Division; André Turcat, his counterpart at Aérospatiale; and Sir George Edwards, Chairman of BAC and leader of the British side of the programme from its inception. Below: The first British-assembled Concorde, prototype 002, taking off from Filton on April 9, 1969.

by being too closely tailored to the specific needs of a single operator. BAC and Aérospatiale could, and did, count themselves fortunate to have the advice and the constructive criticism of major airlines – making up between them a good cross-section of the international air transport market. Their co-operation was invaluable in such areas as performance and economics, noise, interior layout, product support, ground handling and servicing, and maintainability and reliability.

In parallel with design work for the pre-production aircraft, building of the two prototypes, 001 at Toulouse and 002 at Filton, was going forward, although not as rapidly as had been hoped when the programme began in 1965. Some of the problems arose from the fact that this kind of Anglo-French manufacturing collaboration was something new and needed a period for "bedding down." In a sense, the programme was a prototype and a forerunner of better things to come just as the aircraft was. A great part of the delay was also caused by difficulties in getting on-time delivery of equipment and components from outside suppliers, although this was only to be expected, for many suppliers had to mount their own extensive research programmes to develop their products up to the higher standards demanded by the Concorde operational requirement.

Airborne at last
Nevertheless, on a bitterly cold morning in December, 1967, the first prototype, 001, was rolled out from its assembly hall at Toulouse. This first public appearance of the aeroplane was intended, through the medium of TV, newspapers and magazines, to give the world, and in particular the French and British taxpayers, a chance to see Concorde "in the flesh," and in this it was undoubtedly successful. But there was still much work to be done on the aircraft and months of painstaking checks and ground testing were to pass before the Western world's first supersonic transport was ready to make its maiden flight.

From the stage of first cutting metal, it had taken nearly four years to get 001 airborne, a long time admittedly, but taking into account the manifold problems in this new field and the fact that the prototypes were being built, as the production engineers put it, "from the floor up," this was no mean achievement.

Sunday, March 2, 1969 was an emotional day for the men who had planned and built the Concorde. On this first flight, Concorde 001 carried the hopes and aspirations of thousands of people who had contributed to the most ambitious technological project in Europe's history. Airline guests and hundreds of journalists from all over the world had gathered in Toulouse for the occasion. TV cameramen and commentators waited to transmit the flight to millions of viewers throughout Europe and the other five continents.

The flight had had to be postponed the previous day because of heavy mist. On the Sunday morning the mist seemed as heavy, dank and chill as ever. But the meteorologists and the pilot of the Mirage chase plane who took off to report on conditions "up above" were confident that the sun was going to win this time.

And soon it did. Loudspeakers informed the waiting crowd that Concorde's crew were aboard and pre-flight checks in progress. One by one, the four Olympus engines came to life. Fire tenders and rescue vehicles moved into position. Special trucks, fitted with raucous klaxons, raced up and down the runway, scaring away great flocks of birds. The aircraft moved down the perimeter track and turned slowly to line up on the runway.

For what seemed an age the engines rumbled on. Then came a crescendo of sound, and, brakes released, the white aircraft on its tall undercarriage started to move along the runway, slowly at first but gathering speed. A lot of breath was held, a lot of fists tightly clenched. The nose lifted and there was daylight under the nose-wheel.

"She flies, she flies." Millions of televiewers in Britain heard commentator Raymond Baxter's excited shout. In cold blood there may seem something faintly ridiculous about his choice of words – what was Concorde meant to do but fly – but at Toulouse that morning there were not many cold-blooded onlookers.

The crowd watched as she climbed into the blue sky, trailed by her attendant Mirage. Twin plumes of dark smoke marked her passage. She dwindled to a white spot and then was gone. People looked at each other and said trite things to mask the fact that they were deeply moved. It was a short flight, only 40 minutes, but it gave André Turcat and his crew a foretaste of what

flying a Concorde would be like. Afterwards he was to report that the aircraft handled better than the simulator had predicted.

Over on the grandstand the journalists were in touch with the control tower and received word when 001 was on the approach. She came into view and for the first time, they saw that characteristic "sea-bird" swoop in to land. A puff of smoke told that the main bogies were in contact with the runway, the nose-wheel came down, reverse thrust was engaged and the tail parachute broke from its housing to balloon out behind the aircraft.

Safely down! Around the airfield there was a rattle of clapping and applause. Everywhere there were wide smiles of relief. There were lumps in some throats and tears in some eyes, including those of experienced journalists who one would have thought had "seen everything."

"Zéro-zéro-un" taxied to a halt in front of the airport building and passenger stairs were run into position. Within a few minutes the tall figure of Turcat appeared at the top of the steps, followed by his crew. From the crowded terraces there was a roar of cheers and shouts of "Chief." André Turcat looked up and waved briefly to his wife on the airport balcony and then went down to accept smilingly the embraces and the handshakes of the Concorde leaders waiting to congratulate him.

The turn of 002
The first flight of the British-assembled 002 took place on April 9, 1969. Around the airfield at Filton, Bristol, were the same big crowds and, once again, hundreds of newsmen there to tell the world about it. After taking off from Filton, 002, had to land at the RAF station at Fairford, Glos., 50 miles to the north-east, as the factory runway at Filton is less than 9,000ft. long, too short for test flying of Concorde.

As with 001 there was much the same feeling of tension as the pre-flight preparations were made, and much the same emotion as the aircraft raced along the runway and soared into the air. When it landed at Fairford, there were more congratulations, more interviews, more smiles.

Two public occasions, two great days. They had come and gone, and among the flight development teams the feeling was: "We have achieved what the public had every right to expect from us – now we can get on with the job of proving the aeroplane."

SUPERSONIC PROVING

At that time it was foreseen that the flying would be shared among seven Concordes; the two prototypes, the two pre-production aircraft and the first three production-standard aircraft. The first part of the programme would be devoted to development flying to prove the design and to establish the performance characteristics of the aircraft and its systems. When this work had been completed, the programme would continue with certification flying, plus route-proving and endurance flying to demonstrate the aircraft's capabilities as a passenger transport.

All the first four aircraft were purely test vehicles and well described as flying laboratories. Each of the prototypes carried about 12 tons of electronic test instrumentation, much of it specially developed for the purpose. This instrumentation was capable of recording measurements of 3,000 different parameters, including pressures, temperatures, accelerations and attitudes, and the information was recorded on magnetic tape in the aircraft for later analysis in the ground data processing centres. While the aircraft was in flight, certain basic information was continuously telemetered to ground monitoring stations.

In the forward part of the cabin in the prototypes were situated the three panels for the flight observers. At these panels the

The first three Concordes – all "flying laboratories" carrying 12 tons of highly specialised test instrumentation.

observers monitored the behaviour of the aircraft and engine systems, the information being displayed on instruments duplicating those on the flight deck. Once the initial subsonic handling flights had taken place, a start was made on flutter testing, a necessary preliminary to the transonic and supersonic phases of the programme. Flutter is a phenomenon that can be caused when vibrations of a certain frequency in one part of an aircraft structure set off sympathetic vibrations in another part of the structure. If allowed to continue without damping, the interaction can lead to extremely violent vibration and ultimately to structural fracture.

On October 1, 1969 the first supersonic flight by Concorde was made in 001. The

aircraft attained a speed of Mach 1.5 (1,125 mph) and flew supersonically for nine minutes. In general, pilots' reports on the progress of the two prototype aircraft were encouraging. Ground handling characteristics were said to be very good, and there was praise for the ease and precision of control in flight. (This has continued to be a constant feature of pilot reports on Concorde ever since.) When the visor was raised, the absence of noise on the flight deck was said to be impressive, and even, on first experience, rather startling.

It was a measure of the progress made, and of the steady growth of confidence in the aircraft, that it was decided to offer four airline captains the opportunity to fly Concorde 001 early in November, 1969, only seven months after first flight. They were Captain James Andrew of BOAC, Captain Maurice Bernard of Air France, Captain Paul Roitsch of Pan American and Captain Vernon Laursen of TWA.

After two periods in the Concorde flight simulator at Toulouse, each pilot flew 001 up to the speed of Mach 1.2 (850mph), for which it had been cleared by the flight test programme. They were also free to nominate any of the many types of failure that had been investigated, such as an engine failure in flight or a three-engine landing. In a joint report afterwards the pilots said that they found the aircraft pleasant and easy to fly, that the workload was not excessive, and that they foresaw no problems in training airline pilots and engineers to handle the aircraft.

Mach 2

In November, 1970, both aircraft reached Mach 2 (1,350mph) for the first time, within a few days of each other. In the same month, the 300 hours mark was passed. By this time, both aircraft had been fitted with the Olympus 593B engines, which enabled them to maintain Mach 2 cruise speeds over long distances. This new capability of sustained Mach 2 cruise meant that Concorde pilots were moving

The two prototypes flying over countryside typical of their homelands. The smaller picture shows Concorde 001 over the Pyrenees during a test flight from Toulouse, and the larger picture shows Concorde 002 over the green fields of England's West Country.

into a realm of test flying that had hitherto been unexplored. A Concorde's supersonic flight time is much longer than a military aircraft's supersonic dash, and the design problems arising from high structure temperature are more severe.

Most of Concorde's supersonic flying was done over the sea, but special provision had to be made for some overland supersonic flights by 002. For supersonic performance measurements, it was necessary to have a straight line route of about 800 miles, and to safeguard the crew and the aircraft the whole of this route had to be under radar surveillance and within the range of air and ground rescue services. To fulfil these conditions, and at the same time to cause disturbance to the least number of people on the ground, a route was chosen running in a north-south direction over parts of the western coasts of Scotland and Wales, and over Cornwall.

It was made clear that these were test exercises and that it was not expected that more than 50 flights would have to be made, spread over a period of several years. Warning would be given of impending flights, and claims for damage thought to be caused by the aircraft's sonic boom would be considered by the government. As was to be expected, the first flights occasioned a good deal of critical reaction. When first heard, the sonic boom is certainly a startling sound, and, despite the assurances given by the government that this was part of a flight test programme, there were suspicions that this was a plot to "get people used to the noise."

One of the first tests made after Mach 2 had been attained was to check the effect on controllability at this speed of cutting first one engine and then two engines on the same side of the aircraft. Among the gloomy forecasts made by opponents of supersonic passenger transport had been that this type of engine failure would lead to complete loss of control. This test has now been made many times, both with and without auto-rudder, and it has been demonstrated that control is not affected.

The first serious incident in the programme occurred in January, 1971 when 001, flying at supersonic speed, experienced an engine surge which caused one of the movable ramps in the engine air intake to break free. Metal fragments were ingested into the engine, and considerable damage

was caused, but all this damage was contained within the engine casing. The damaged engine was shut down and the aircraft returned on three engines to Toulouse where it made a normal landing.

An intensive investigation was made of the incident and its causes, and corrective design action was put in hand to prevent a recurrence. To uncover potential hazards and to eliminate them is one of the main purposes of a flight development programme. This is why, during the development programme, the aircraft is deliberately pushed beyond the limits of its normal flight envelope, and why the most mathematically unlikely combinations of failures are set up for study purposes.

Later in 1971, 001 made the first intercontinental Concorde flights when it flew from Toulouse to Dakar on May 25 and from Dakar to Le Bourget, Paris, on May 26 for the opening of the Paris Air Show. The Dakar-Paris flight of 2,500 miles was flown in 2hr. 52min., including 2hr. 7min. at supersonic speed.

On September 4, Concorde 001 set off from Toulouse on the longest sortie it had so far made from base, a demonstration tour of South America. In the space of 15 days, the aircraft visited Rio de Janeiro, Sao Paulo

Below: This view of Concorde shows to advantage its exceptionally clean wing, devoid of air brakes and spoilers, but with three servo-controlled elevons on each wing. Right: Concorde over Rio de Janeiro on its first South American visit in September, 1971.

and Buenos Aires, and made 16 flights. Nearly a hundred South American guests were flown at Mach 2 speeds, and 001 proved itself perfectly capable of fitting into the normal traffic control patterns at airports, even in the very adverse weather conditions experienced on several days during the tour.

It so happened that during 1971, prototype 001 had performed most of the newsworthy feats but the turn of 002 was to come. Throughout that year both aircraft had together built up the total of flying hours, extended the frontiers of knowledge, sorted out problems and test-flown the solutions. In short, they had got on with their exacting and essential task.

The year 1971, when Concorde was spreading its inter-continental wings, saw the end of the rival American SST project. It was finally halted in March by the Senate's refusal to vote further funds. Much of the "credit" for killing the American SST was claimed by the environmentalists, but in retrospect it appears that the real causes of its demise were technical and financial. The emotive crusade of the protest groups provided political justification for action that would have had to be taken anyway.

First passenger reaction
The elimination of American competition in the supersonic travel market did not, however, cause any elation in BAC and Aérospatiale. On balance, it was regarded as bad news rather than good. Leaders of the Concorde project felt that, in the political battles they could see ahead, it

Above: Concorde 002, the second prototype, on a test flight. Left: Concorde 01, the first pre-production aircraft, photographed from its chase Canberra when landing at Fairford.

would have been useful to have an American SST following close behind. Events were to prove this feeling well-founded.

In addition to the South American guests, a handful of other privileged people flew in the two Concorde prototypes during 1971 and so became the first passengers, apart from the test observers and development engineers, to experience flight at twice the speed of sound. Among the first was President Pompidou of France who flew in 001 from Paris to Toulouse, taking in a supersonic section over the Bay of Biscay en route. Later in the programme, the Duke of Edinburgh was to fly in 002 and to take over the controls at Mach 2 for a time.

Press reaction
At the Paris Air Show in May and June, 1971, a series of demonstration flights was made with 001, carrying government representatives, airline executives and influential aviation journalists. One of the latter, Robert Hotz, editor of the well-known American magazine *Aviation Week and Space Technology* described his flight in an editorial in the next issue of the magazine: "The most sensational aspect of flying as a passenger at Mach 2 in a supersonic transport is that there are no sensations whatsoever that differ from those in the current generation of subsonic jets . . .

"The only unusual internal noise comes during take-off briefly from engine rumble. The cabin noise level without full airline-style sound-proofing is about equal to that of a current subsonic jet with only a slight increase near the aft section. Cabin pressurization maintains a constant 6,500ft. environment even during supersonic climb and descent. During Mach 2 maneuvers, only the changing color of the sky informs the passengers of major banking turns. It is possible and pleasant to walk around during all flight regimes. Stewards will have no trouble serving martinis and meals. Passengers will find no difficulty consuming them. They will just have to drink a little faster – New York will be only a few hours away."

002 also took its quota of passengers on flights from the Fairford flight test centre, either over the Bay of Biscay or the North Sea. These 1,000-mile flights took about an hour and a half and came to be referred to colloquially as "trips round the bay."

Since those early flights, one has heard many first-time Concorde passengers trying to put their reactions into words. Some have been eloquent and have spoken of a triumph of the human spirit. Some have been tongue-tied – and yet have been eloquent in their own way, like the Frenchman who came down the gangway and said briefly, "C'est impossible, mais . . ."

World tour preparations
By early 1972, plans were being worked out for the most exacting overseas tour ever undertaken by a development aircraft. The proposal was to send Concorde 002 on a 46,000 miles journey to the Middle East, the Far East and Australia, a 30-day trip that would call for weeks of preparation. It came to be known as the "world tour", a description that was not precisely accurate since it was a halfway-round-the-world-and-back-again tour.

This ambitious exercise was regarded as a logical extension of the flight development programme to date, although there were those who thought that it would have been preferable to wait until one of the later and more advanced aircraft was available. This school of thought regarded it as "counter-productive" (that useful piece of jargon) to send a prototype Concorde so far afield. Because it was an early-development aircraft, they argued, it would give a misleading impression of Concorde in the countries it visited. Its engines were noisier and more smoky than those to be fitted in the series-production aircraft. It lacked the range of the later types and could therefore not demonstrate the full capability of Concorde over the long inter-continental routes.

There was much force in these arguments; that was conceded even by those who were for going ahead with the tour. But they believed that 002, prototype though it was, would make a dramatic impact wherever it was seen for the first time. It would demonstrate the great time-savings of supersonic passenger flight to the opinion-formers and the policy-makers. It would carry the British and the French flags all over the world. Its shortcomings could be admitted and explained.

Concorde 002 at Fairford, being prepared for its 46,000-miles demonstration tour of the Middle East, Far East and Australia in 1972.

The 1972 tour took in Singapore . . .

. . . then Manila in the Philippines . . .

. . . and then Tokyo's Haneda airport.

Application was made for the aircraft to operate supersonically through the airspace of a number of countries along the route. Agreement was reached for such operation in the Middle East, Indonesia and Australia on the understanding that the permission was granted on an experimental basis and that the flights would be made along carefully defined corridors. Most of the civil aviation authorities in the countries concerned made arrangements to monitor the Concorde sonic boom.

Much of the preparatory work was devoted to the logistics problem. After leaving Fairford, 002 would be visiting 14 airports in 12 countries; ground crews and specialised equipment had to be stationed everywhere in advance and spares had to be on hand. The fact that the British government provided logistics support in the shape of an RAF Belfast transport aircraft and a VC10 was seized upon by the ever-watchful critics:

"So much for the makers' claims about Concorde's reliability, it cannot leave its base without support aircraft going along to carry spares for it."

This was a more than usually pointless piece of carping. In airline service, Concorde spares would, like those of all other current types, be held at maintenance bases all over the world, and to cope with emergencies, airlines would have spares pooling arrangements. But, although the criticism was not taken too seriously, it was a reminder, if any were needed, that this Concorde tour would take place in the limelight of public attention. Concorde was being shown to the world, and if anything went wrong with the aircraft, the world would soon get to know.

At last came departure day, June 2. The first stop was Athens after a two-and-a-half-hour subsonic flight across Europe. Crowds began to gather and the airport terraces were soon crammed with cheerful people. On the airfield blue-overalled Concorde ground crews had established amiable contact with the local crews, a feat they managed to achieve everywhere they went. Aircraft came and went, and in the distance the Mediterranean sparkled in the sunshine.

A promising start
Now watches were being consulted. Time she was in sight, was the unspoken thought. It was the first port of call and a good beginning would be an omen. Technologists, being members of the human race, are no more rational about these things than

the rest of us. And there, suddenly, was 002, a speck in the blue sky which set the spectators chattering and pointing. There followed a scene that, with variations was to become very familiar in the next few weeks.

A smooth landing and an informal welcome for the disembarking passengers as the ground crews in the background bustled into action; a Press conference in the airport lounge, with Air Minister Michael Heseltine and flight test director Brian Trubshaw fielding the questions and giving details of the flight; TV interviews; telex messages to base; a lot of bustle but remarkably little confusion. All the detailed planning was beginning to pay off.

In what seemed a remarkably short time, the aircraft was taking off for the next leg, another subsonic flight to Tehran where it was due to be based for three days. Here, to greet it, were more crowds, more sunshine, more work. Next day, on the first of two supersonic demonstration flights, Concorde was honoured by the presence of the Shah of Iran, who occupied the left-hand pilot's seat throughout the flight. This was one of the routes over which special permission had been given for supersonic flying, and after the flight the Shah was complimentary about the calmness and comfort of Mach 2 flying in Concorde. He went further and announced that the national airline Iran Air would be buying Concorde. It was a heartening start to the world tour.

On June 6, the aircraft flew to Bombay, via Bahrain, where it made a three-hour stop to allow time for an inspection by the Ruler, Sheik Essa Bin Sulman Al-Khalifa. On the Bahrain-Bombay sector, 002 had its first chance to prove that it could cut normal flight schedules in half by doing the journey in just over two hours.

On to the Far East
An overnight stop was made at Bombay; a brief halt, but it was planned to stay there for several days on the return journey. Next morning's flight across the Bay of Bengal at Mach 2 brought Concorde to Bangkok in 2 hr. 34 min., cutting an hour and a half off the best subsonic time, and after the short stop at Bangkok, the aircraft flew subsonically across Malaysia to Singapore.

Singapore's Prime Minister, Lee Kuan Yew, inspected 002, and his young son and daughter were among the passengers on the first supersonic demonstration flight on June 9. It was at Singapore that, for the first and only time on the tour, technical trouble prevented the aircraft from stick-

ing to its extremely tight schedule. A snag on the weather radar held the aircraft up for ten hours, and, as it was impracticable to delay arrival at Tokyo, a third Singapore demonstration flight had to be cancelled. However, a promise was given (and kept) that this flight would be reinstated on the return journey.

Environment conscious Japan
Singapore to Tokyo was flown in two supersonic sectors, with an overnight stop at Manila to give the Philippines a sight of the Concorde. Flying time for the journey of about 3,300 miles was just under four hours, again half the best subsonic scheduled time. Tokyo had been regarded as one of the most critical points on the tour. Haneda is one of the busiest international airports in the world, and this first visit by Concorde would be a real test of its ability to fit into a dense traffic pattern. The Japanese are now among the most environment-conscious people in the world, and in this respect Concorde's performance would be carefully studied.

Three landings and three take-offs at Tokyo proved to the airport authorities and air traffic control that Concorde is just another efficient subsonic aeroplane in these conditions. There was the expected newspaper criticism of the smoky exhausts and the engine noise level, but there was also widespread acceptance of the fact that the engine manufacturers were working to improve the Olympus in both these areas. On the first of two Mach 2 flights, members of the Japanese Diet accompanied the chairman and the vice-president of Japan Air Line. Tokyo businessmen and officials also of the national airline inspected 002 on the ground, taking great interest in the electronic test instrumentation.

Heading south on June 15, 002 reached Darwin in a little over four hours' flying time from Tokyo. Arrival at Darwin was delayed for about 90 minutes by the need to replace an air conditioning valve at the Manila transit stop, but this was to be the last significant delay on the whole tour.

After a day's servicing, Concorde flew to Sydney on June 17, along a route that had been carefully planned by the Australian Department of Civil Aviation to avoid townships and Aboriginal reserves. The flight corridor passed near Alice Springs where the boom was measured and its effects studied. It was found that little disturbance was caused to animals, birds or to local inhabitants.

The tour organisers had been warned to expect considerable environmental opposition at Sydney, and groups of protesters had gathered near the Kingsford Smith international airport. They were far outnumbered, however, by the crowds of Australians who had come along in their traditional "give it a go" spirit to see Concorde for themselves. On the approach to land, one of the Concorde pilots saw some of the young protesters throw aside their placards and start waving at the "monster" they had come to protest about.

For all the next day the aircraft was on

Below: Monsoon weather at Bombay. From Darwin (left), Concorde made the first supersonic passenger flight across Australia, landing at Sydney (right).

Concorde at Dhahran, Saudi Arabia.

The Saudi-Arabian royal party.

view in front of the airport terminal buildings, and thousands of people came to walk round the barricade surrounding 002, taking photographs and asking innumerable questions. There was plenty of typically caustic Australian humour, but there was also genuine admiration, often summed up in the words, "She's beaut," and more than one expatriate British family told Concorde men how good it was to see something from the old country they could feel a pride in.

Mr William McMahon, then Prime Minister of Australia, and his wife came to inspect Concorde. Government ministers, Qantas executives and airport officials flew on the two supersonic "demos" from Sydney, the second of which took the aircraft, after a wide sweep over the Tasman Sea, to Melbourne. Here, two more flights were made and the names of more distinguished passengers added to the list.

Back home
Melbourne was the turning-point. From there on 002 would be homeward bound. In the 20 days journeying from Fairford, the outlook of the Concorde support party had undergone a transformation. The "fingers crossed" attitude of the first few days had given way to complete confidence in the aircraft and her crew. All the reservations and the doubts were forgotten. Most important of all, perhaps, was the knowledge that everywhere Concorde went the ordinary men and women in the street were "on our side."

On June 22, Concorde flew back along the same supersonic corridor to Darwin, and then on the following day to Singapore where the promised demonstration flight was organised. Taking off from Singapore on June 25, the aircraft flew to Bangkok and on to Bombay. The crossing of the Bay of Bengal was made supersonically at 54,000ft., just above the monsoon storm-clouds. To cross India, 002 slowed to subsonic speed although it is doubtful whether its boom would have been heard among the thunderstorms.

The next leg was to Dhahran in Saudi Arabia where, on a demonstration flight, HRH Prince Turki Bin Abdul Aziz and high Saudi officials enjoyed their first experience of flight at twice the speed of sound. At the next stop, Beirut, the last supersonic demonstration flight of the tour was made for government officials and executives of Middle East Airlines. The flight from Beirut to Toulouse on June 30 included the longest oversea sector of the tour, and the 2,400 miles was flown in 2 hr.

19 min. Beirut–Toulouse is not at present an airline sector, but it might well become one in future Concorde operations.

Precisely at noon on July 1, Concorde 002 landed at London Heathrow, spot on time after a well-nigh faultless month of intensive worldwide operation in a variety of environments and extremes of climate. The last Press conference was held, the last questions answered – and the general verdict was, "Good show." Thousands of people travelled to Heathrow on the Sunday to see Concorde, and on Monday morning came an unannounced visit by the Queen and Princess Anne, a signal honour to mark the conclusion of the tour.

By the end of 1975, when it is due to enter service, Concorde will have been under development for 13 years. That is about twice the length of time forecast when the project was begun. Those predictions were made in good faith, however. That the problems ahead proved far more complex than had been visualised is part of the risk that nations take when they launch on a project as advanced as Concorde. After all the Soviet Union, with their vast aerospace industry and impressive achievements in space, have nevertheless taken much the same time over their SST project.

The fare structure
The long development period has created special problems for Concorde. Air travel has changed dramatically in the intervening years. The slow growth of business traffic came to a halt around 1967. Stagnation in the business travel market was accompanied by a steady growth of leisure traffic as promotional fares – filling seats by enabling tourists, students and parties to preferential rates on giving fairly long notice – became more and more attractive.

By the early 1970s, the promotional "tail" was wagging the full-fare "dog." On the North Atlantic routes it was calculated that business travellers, representing about 30 per cent of the total traffic, were producing about 60 per cent of the total revenue. For scheduled airline operators, another factor in the deteriorating situation was the rapid increase in competition from charter operators over the last ten years or so.

In 1975, therefore, the situation is totally different from that in 1962 when Concorde's manufacturers were making the first market studies. Long-haul air traffic has been transformed from mainly business travel to a mix of leisure and business with the numerically smaller proportion of business

passengers providing the greater part of the revenue. In addition, since the introduction of the wide-bodied Jumbo jets, airlines have faced a problem of over-capacity far exceeding anything previously known.

How has the transformation of the market affected the saleability of Concorde? Concorde's greatest asset is its speed, its ability to get you there in half the time, but there was a practical restriction on the use of that speed, the sonic boom. A detailed study of the world's long-distance route structures and the volume of traffic they carried, showed that about 73 per cent of all inter-continental seat-miles were produced over the oceans and, with minor re-routing, another seven per cent could be added to this total. That was reassuring, for there is no sonic boom problem over the seas. (On its world tours, Concorde has overflown thousands of ships of all types and there has never been any adverse report on its boom.)

Gradually there evolved what came to be known as the "mixed-fleet" philosophy. Hitherto, the main classification of air transport has been the standard of cabin service offered. For a premium of about 60 per cent over the economy fare, the first-class air traveller gets rather more elbow room and leg room, free drink and more elaborate meals, *but* (and this is the crux of the Concorde philosophy) he does not get to his destination any quicker than the economy traveller. One flies to save time, but the first-class traveller does not save any more time in return for his higher fare.

Time is money
In introducing Concorde, the operator could for the first time offer the first-class traveller something for his money; hours of extra time. Those who travel first class are not usually fare-conscious, but they are time-conscious and would welcome those extra hours. Many of the economy-class business travellers could also be expected to opt for Concorde. For them or their companies there would be a simple question to be asked: is the value of x hours of Mr A's time worth more than the Concorde fare premium? And if the answer were "yes", then he would travel Concorde.

What is needed, according to the mixed-fleet philosophers, is that the big subsonic jets are also configured as single-class vehicles. At present, every first-class seat in these aircraft is occupying space equivalent to about two-and-a-half subsonic seats, and this uneconomic use of space is one reason why the wide-bodied jets have not fulfilled the early promises of reduced operating costs. If they were laid out as economy class throughout, their operating economics would be greatly improved.

On suitable routes, the two types would provide complementary services, and each would be operating in a role for which it was designed, the supersonic aircraft offering the speed and convenience that the business traveller requires and the subsonic aircraft the low-cost travel that the leisure market requires. Whereas in the past the two stimuli to traffic growth – higher speed and lower fares – had been provided by one new type of aircraft, now they would be supplied by two separate types.

Making what appeared to be reasonable assumptions about the load factors which might be expected for Concorde and the wide-bodied jets operating in harness in this way, the supersonic salesmen were able to demonstrate that the overall profitability of the mixed fleet would be better than that of an all-subsonic fleet with the same total seating capacity. To achieve this result, it could well be necessary to reduce frequencies on the subsonic services, but this could be done without causing hardship to the leisure traveller (subsequent economic pressures have indeed compelled airlines to reduce frequencies and to coordinate services).

It was a well-reasoned argument, and if it could be proved, the end result would be better service, not just for the air travel élite, but for the whole range of passengers by air. This would spike one of the main criticisms: that Concorde would benefit only the privileged few.

Above: HRH Princess Anne, seen in Concorde with Sir George Edwards, made a supersonic flight in 002. Left: At Bangkok, a perfect illustration of the "mixed-fleet concept."

Aérospatiale and BAC decided to mount a professionally-conducted survey in the USA. Nearly 300 business travellers, all of whom had made at least two overseas trips in the previous year, were interviewed at New York, Chicago, Los Angeles and San Francisco. An important aspect of this survey is that it covered the reactions to both single-class and mixed-class Concorde cabin layouts.

The survey showed that on Transatlantic and Trans-Pacific routes, more than 90 per cent of first-class travellers would switch to Concorde at first-class fares, and, even at first-class plus 50 per cent, 85 per cent would still travel Concorde. On the West Coast-Hawaii route, there was more resistance to this higher premium fare, but if a mixed-class layout were used on this route many present first-class travellers would elect to fly Concorde economy and a high total switch to Concorde would still be achieved.

As expected, economy-class travellers showed themselves more sensitive to fare levels, but even so, there would be a change-over to Concorde by more than 30 per cent of business economy travellers on the North Atlantic routes and by more than 50 per cent on the Pacific routes. Only a very small number of those questioned commented adversely on Concorde's relatively small cabin, and the great majority clearly regarded this as being more than offset by the time savings. On the basis of replies from these travellers it was estimated that the introduction of Concorde would lead to an increase in business travel of between 13 and 17 per cent, depending on fare level.

These results confirmed the previous BAC-Aérospatiale estimates of market penetration arrived at by statistical analysis, and they clearly supported the mixed-fleet philosophical arguments. A market survey is, of course, always open to criticism on the size of the sample and the framing of the questions, and this survey was not entirely accepted in airline circles. However, the results were agreed to be a significant pointer to the acceptability of supersonic travel. In 1975 another survey was conducted among Japanese business travellers with the close co-operation of Japan Air Lines, and the results were almost exactly the same as in the American survey – the passenger appeal of speed is irresistible and there will be a demand for Concorde travel even at premium fares.

THE END OF THE BEGINNING

In July, 1972, BOAC and Air France signed contracts for a total of nine Concordes, an event described by Sir George Edwards, chairman of BAC, in the Churchillean phrase as "the end of the beginning." Six months later, Pan American and TWA decided to cancel their options, an event that was hailed in some quarters as the beginning of the end.

BOAC had already announced that it planned to operate Concorde on routes to the USA, the Far East, Australia and South Africa. Air France had not made any public statement of its intentions, but it was expected that a service from Paris to Rio de Janeiro would be one of its first objectives. A ministerial statement in Parliament gave

the information that the cost to BOAC of their five Concordes, including spares, was £125 millions. It was a heavy capital commitment, but the high unit cost of the aircraft has to be considered in relation to its unit productivity; each Concorde will be capable of carrying more passengers across the North Atlantic in a year than an ocean liner of the size of the *Queen Elizabeth II*.

Both BOAC and Air France firmly denied suggestions that their contracts had been negotiated under any form of government duress. Nevertheless, it was generally accepted that the acid test of Concorde's marketability would come when the leading American carriers were required to decide on their options. In the meantime,

there were two other heartening developments for the Concorde builders.

First, during a visit to London, the Shah of Iran reaffirmed that it was Iran Air's intention to order two Concordes, with a third on option. He said: "This is something that is finished and done. The actual date and delivery will be discussed later." (At the time of writing, several years later, the contract negotiations with Iran Air are in the final stages and the outcome probably depends more on political decisions elsewhere in the world than on the technical and commercial qualities of the aircraft.)

The second encouraging development was the addition of the Chinese national civil aviation corporation to the list of

potential Concorde customers. After lengthy exchanges between France and China, a preliminary purchase agreement for the supply of two Concordes from the Toulouse assembly line was signed in Paris on July 24. A second agreement, for delivery of a third aircraft from the BAC line, was signed in Peking a month later.

Thus, over the space of two months, contracts and preliminary purchase agreements had been signed, representing a total commitment to Concorde of several hundred millions of pounds. Market prospects suddenly seemed brighter, and once again a slightly unreal euphoria was being generated in some quarters. Before long, however, a chill wind began to blow from the direction of the USA. One of the conditions of the first option agreements had been that, within six months of contract signature by BOAC or Air France, the option-holders had to reach a final decision on whether or not to convert their options into firm orders. Now BOAC and Air France *had* signed and, in a phrase then current, "the clock had begun to tick."

"Soon there will be only two kinds of airlines," say BAC and Aérospatiale's advertisements. "Those with Concorde and those which take twice as long." Air France (above) and British Airways will be the first airlines to operate Concorde.

Pan Am and TWA
The main sales effort of the manufacturers was now concentrated on Pan American and TWA. If these, the two biggest long-haul operators in the world, could be persuaded to endorse Concorde by converting options into orders, many other airlines would follow their example. If they cancelled, it was likely that other airlines would do the same and decide to wait.

For the Concorde team, the stakes could hardly have been higher and the game could hardly have been played at a worse time. After a long reign as the most successful airline in the world, Pan American had had a series of disastrously unprofitable years. Some of the troubles had been caused by an over-extension of operations

in the "fat" years, but the main problem was the excess capacity resulting from the heavy investment in wide-bodied jets. In January, 1973, TWA were also running at a loss, although not to the same extent.

Negotiations went on almost under the eyes of the world news media, a fact that added to the pressure on both sides. "It was like working in a goldfish bowl," was the way one BAC man put it. As was to be expected, the main discussions centred around the economics of the aircraft. The performance guarantees that the makers were prepared to offer would probably have been found acceptable but there was a difference of opinion on the likely revenue-earning capacity of the aircraft.

Both airlines considered that the BAC-Aérospatiale estimates of the business traffic switch to Concorde were over-optimistic, and there was disagreement over the predictions of Concorde operating costs. In the process of negotiating a sale of aircraft equipment, differences of this kind are not unusual, but on this occasion the gulf between the two sides was wide

enough to represent the difference between a profitable and a loss-making operation. And, despite a vigorous and highly professional marketing campaign, the gulf proved to be unbridgeable. On January 31, 1973, the last day of the six months period, Pan American announced that it had decided to cancel its options. Within an hour, TWA announced a similar decision.

"Not a mortal blow"
In its statement, Pan American said that its studies indicated that the "aeroplane will be capable of scheduled supersonic service," but that it would require substantially higher fares than today's and therefore did not satisfy the airlines' future requirements. TWA commended the technical achievements of the Concorde programme, but said that the first priority in the use of capital resources must be given to the improvement and expansion of its subsonic fleet.

Neither airline excluded the possibility that its interest in Concorde might be revived in the future. Pan American said that they would "maintain an open door to the manufacturers should they have any new proposals they wished to make." TWA said that they would maintain an interest in future developments of the programme and "would be available for discussions in the event of significant improvements in the viability of the airplane."

To Concorde supporters these pie-in-the-sky statements did little to soften their disappointment. Some people affected to see in the cancellations, coming so close together, a deep-laid plot to kill a European project that appeared to threaten American supremacy in the long-haul aircraft market. This supposition might have been a small sop to national pride but there was no evidence to support it. The decision to cancel had been taken on the airlines' assessment, however misguided it might be, of the economic viability of Concorde. It was no

Left: Passenger after passenger has said that, without the Machmeter in the cabin, they could not have told when Concorde had "gone through the sound barrier." Right: Concorde's speed provided scientists with a unique opportunity to observe a total eclipse of the sun for a record 74 minutes.

consolation to reflect how often airlines had been wrong in such assessments.

With his flair for the down-to-earth phrase, Sir George Edwards said: "This is a hell of a setback but it is not a mortal blow." It was a time for taking the long view, and neither the British nor the French government showed any sign of wavering in their support for the project. There would have to be some re-thinking on the manufacturing programme, but this would be directed towards a slow-down rather than a run-down. As expected, other operators, notably American Airlines and Eastern Airlines, followed Pan American and TWA in cancelling their options.

Although Concorde supporters made a speedy re-adjustment to the new situation, the psychological effects of the series of cancellations were depressing in the extreme. It could be argued that options were not orders and that it was wrong to regard a cancelled option in the same light as an order lost to a rival manufacturer. Yet whatever gloss was put upon the situation, the cold fact remained that Concorde had, for the time being, been rejected by a number of the world's most experienced operators.

For critics of the project, the option setbacks provided excellent ammunition. They concentrated on the airline doubts about the economic viability of the aircraft, but here again Sir George Edwards gave a clearcut answer to the doubters. He pointed out that on British Airways's own estimates of Concorde operating costs and Concorde fare levels, the aircraft would break even

(including repayment of capital) at a load factor of 55–60 per cent. Since British Airways was thinking of a cabin layout with seating for around 100 passengers, that meant that Concorde would start to make a profit at an average load of about 55 passengers.

Even among the opposition – or, at least among those sections of the opposition with any knowledge of the aviation business – there was general agreement that Concorde would attract much more than a 55–60 per cent load factor. In the past even a modest increase in cruise speed had abstracted traffic from slower vehicles – and Concorde was going to *halve* existing flight times.

American airlines' public criticisms of Concorde economics probably masked private fears about the revolutionary effect that the introduction of a supersonic airliner would have on the whole field of air transport. On its own account, Concorde could be operated at a profit; business travellers would be prepared, as one of them put it, "to pay real money for a real time saving." But what would be the effect on the economics of the subsonic fleet?

The makers' answer to this question was the mixed-fleet philosophy. But the validity of this new approach to airline marketing could not be demonstrated until Concorde had gone into service.

Progress report
For the thousands of Frenchmen and Britons engaged on the Concorde project, the years 1973 and 1974 were a test of endurance, nerve, and teamwork. In the machine shops and on the assembly lines, in the laboratories and on the test rigs, in the computer centres and in the offices, the work went on. Sales teams toured the world, keeping airlines informed of progress.

The flight test programme also went ahead. The first significant event was the maiden flight from Toulouse on January 10, 1973 of pre-production aircraft 02, the fourth Concorde to fly. It was significant because this was the first aircraft to be fitted with the new Mk 602-type Olympus 593 engines with the re-designed combustion chamber. As the aircraft took off, it could be seen that the smoke problem had indeed been cured. Instead of the twin black·trails the prototypes had left behind them, there was only the faintest haze.

At about the same time, Concorde 002 began what was to prove to be a lengthy search for natural ice. Tests of the de-icing system had been made by flying Concorde behind a water tanker aircraft fitted with spraying equipment, but to meet the full requirements of the certification authorities it was necessary to demonstrate that the system could cope with a two-inch build-up of natural ice. 002 made a number of flights from Fairford in search of ice and later moved to Prestwick for further tests in more northerly latitudes, but without encountering severe enough conditions.

As if to underline the wide scope of the test programme, 002 was soon assigned to an entirely different task when it flew to South Africa for "hot and high" trials at Jan Smuts airport, Johannesburg. This airport is about 5,500ft. above sea level, and in January and February the temperature often exceeds 80°F. It is therefore a good location for establishing the effects of altitude and temperature on Concorde's airfield performance. Twenty-eight test

flights were made, and the results obtained were within one per cent of prediction.

Because of its capacity for sustained supersonic flight, Concorde has been able to make important contributions to scientific knowledge. On June 30, 1973, for example, Concorde 001 provided scientists with the longest-ever sight of a total eclipse of the sun. Taking off from Las Palmas, it chased the moon's shadow at twice the speed of sound across Africa to the vicinity of Lake Tchad. Seven scientists from French, British and American universities on board were able to take full advantage of 74 minutes of continuous observation of the eclipse. This record is likely to stand for 177 years as no eclipse of similar duration will occur until the year 2150.

For the Paris Air Show of 1973, marred by the crash of the Soviet TU 144 on the final day, pre-production aircraft 02 had the rear section of its cabin specially fitted out for VIP passenger travel. Typical French design flair was shown in the luxurious leather seating and the decor, and the final touch was provided by a wall-mounted Machmeter enabling passengers to check

The need to prove Concorde in every type of operating environment has led to tests being carried out at many airports overseas. The prototype 002 is seen here at Johannesburg's Jan Smuts Airport during "hot and high" trials .

on the aircraft's speed. After the somewhat spartan interiors of the prototypes, 02 was a revelation and it gave many influential visitors to the Show a foretaste of what supersonic travel will really be like.

The year 1973 saw the effective completion of the two prototypes' contribution to the flight development programme. They had successfully fulfilled their purpose in establishing the basic design characteristics of Concorde and making the first exploration of the flight envelope. One of 002's last programmed operations was a further series of hot airfield trials at the Spanish airbase of Torrejon, near Madrid. Concorde 001 was honourably retired to a French aviation museum at Le Bourget, but at the time of writing the final disposition of 002, which remains in an airworthy condition, has not been decided.

American visit

In September, 1973 Concorde made its first visit to the USA in response to an invitation to attend the inauguration of the new Dallas-Fort Worth airport. The first leg of the route took 02 from Paris to Caracas, a distance of nearly 5,200 miles. This was flown, including a refuelling stop at Las Palmas, in 6hr. 25min., thus cutting some five hours off the best subsonic scheduled time. During its four-day stay in Texas, Concorde 02 made supersonic demonstration flights over the Gulf of Mexico and

Concorde at Dallas/Fort Worth, Texas.

The Anglo-French airliner at Caracas.

proved to be the outstanding attraction in the flying displays which formed part of the airport dedication ceremonies.

On Sunday, September 23, 02 flew to Dulles airport, Washington, D.C., and because of its ability to cruise at a higher subsonic speed than the conventional jets, staked a claim to be the world's fastest subsonic airliner by cutting 20 minutes off the Dallas-Dulles normal flight time.

In December, 1973 the first production-standard Concorde took to the air. On its maiden flight from Toulouse, it was airborne for three hours and flew supersonically for the better part of an hour. Although it was built essentially to the same standard as aircraft destined for airline service, this Concorde still carried a substantial quantity of special test equipment and was scheduled to continue flight development work for some years to come.

Performance and technical trials

Over the first months of 1974, the four Concordes now engaged on the flight test programme flew to various overseas destinations on special missions. In January, Concorde 01 spent a week in Tangier, which was used as a base for a series of flights into the cold high-altitude regions over the South Atlantic. Low temperatures at high altitude proved the most testing conditions for the variable engine air intakes, and this programme produced satisfactory and consistent results.

As part of any certification programme, a new aircraft type has to undergo *cold soak* tests on the ground to demonstrate that it can be operated and maintained in low temperature conditions. For this purpose, Concorde 02 flew from Toulouse to Fairbanks, Alaska in February; the flight taking less than six hours, with a refuelling stop at Keflavik, Iceland. The aircraft was left standing in the open at night with temperatures dropping to below −44°C and was then put through a series of systems functioning tests which it passed without difficulty. Local engineers were impressed by the ease of engine starts and the ruggedness of the Concorde systems.

In May, Concorde 02 embarked on a programme of flights on North and South Atlantic routes designed to prove its ability to operate in typical airline conditions and to airline standards of regularity. In the ten days from May 27 to June 5, ten flights were made between Paris and Rio de Janeiro, with a transit stop at Dakar en route. The performance figures speak for themselves. Planned time for the single journey was 6hr. 10min. and the achieved average was 6hr. 6min.; the planned transit stop time was 50 minutes and the achieved average was 44 minutes; and the planned total trip time was seven hours against an achieved average of 6hr. 50min. All departures were performed within five minutes of the published schedules. This section of the programmes ended with a day return trip to Rio. On June 5, Concorde 02 left Paris at 7.21a.m. and returned 9.58p.m., having flown 12,000 miles and logged another nine hours of supersonic flight.

Racing against a Jumbo

At the invitation of the Massachusetts Port Authority, 02 flew to Boston on June 13 to take part in the dedication of the new John Volpe international terminal. The Paris-Boston crossing set a new record at 3hr. 9min., and this was followed the next day by a rapid return flight to Miami.

On June 17, 02 showed its paces to spectacular effect. It took off from Boston at 8.22a.m. and, at almost the same time, an Air France Boeing 747 left Paris en route for Boston. The two aircraft crossed when the 747 was 620 miles out of Paris and 02 was nearly 2,400 miles out of Boston. Despite the Concorde turn-round time at Paris being extended to 68 minutes because one passenger could not be found, at the end of its return flight it landed at Boston 11 minutes ahead of the 747. Five hundred businessmen from Brazil, the USA, West Germany, France, and Britain sampled and approved of supersonic travel on these two series of flights, and an estimated crowd of 100,000 people came to see the aircraft while it was on view at Boston, causing the biggest traffic jams ever known there.

In August came the counterpart of the Fairbanks trials when the second production aircraft set off for engineering systems tests in the tropical conditions of the Gulf. It flew from Heathrow to Tehran and thence to Bahrain, where it was fitted out with 100 passenger seats, many of which had special seat-back probes to check on temperature distribution.

"Cold soak" trials of Concorde were carried out in the harsh and exacting environment of Fairbanks airport, Alaska, where the second pre-production aircraft, 02, successfully demonstrated that Arctic temperatures as low as −44°C presented no operating problems.

Above: Concorde at San Francisco, one of the major Pacific Coast "gateways" into the USA. Opposite: 02 at Bogotá, one of the world's highest airports.

In the technical trials that followed Concorde's air conditioning system was thoroughly tested and its efficiency proven. Periods of *hot soak* on the ground were followed by flights with increasing numbers of passengers, culminating in a full 100-passenger load. During the flights, there were simulated failures of one or more elements of the air conditioning system. Even with only two of the four elements functioning, it was possible to maintain cabin temperature at a comfortable level.

In a nine-day demonstration tour in October, Concorde 02 once more underlined the point that it and the other Concordes had already made: that the age of supersonic travel is about to begin. The tour took 02 from Heathrow to Mexico City, via Gander (the first landing by Concorde on Canadian soil), and then on to San Francisco, Anchorage, Los Angeles, Lima, Bogotá, Caracas and Las Palmas to Paris. As well as being a convincing marketing demonstration, the tour added to the build-up of practical experience, as it included operations into seven unfamiliar airports, among them the high-altitude fields at

Mexico City and Bogotá, and two of the major gateways into the United States, San Francisco and Los Angeles.

Naturally, it was the show-piece tours such as this that made the headlines, but it is fitting to wind up this 1973–74 progress report with a brief mention of some less spectacular test operations which nevertheless made essential contributions to the main objective: qualifying the aircraft for the grant of a certificate of airworthiness.

In November and December, the first two production Concordes were engaged on certification trials at Casablanca, an airfield with important advantages for this kind of flight development programme. Part of the trials were concerned with engine intake functioning and Casablanca provides easy access to the cold high-altitude regions in which the intake system is most severely tested. Another aspect of the trials was airfield noise measurement,

and the unobstructed terrain around the Casablanca airfield is ideal for this.

And the search for that elusive natural ice was finally crowned with success. Concorde 01, operating in December from the Moses Lake airfield in the American north-west State of Washington, was at last able to achieve the required two-inch accretion of ice on the wing leading edge – and to demonstrate the de-icing system's efficiency.

These two years of intensive flight testing carried the certification programme well along the way towards completion, leaving the route-proving and endurance flying in the summer of 1975 as the final phase. When the great mass of test data acquired in the flight development programme had been analysed, every aspect of the aircraft's performance could be defined in specific detail. Now marketing discussion with airlines could be conducted on the basis of established fact rather than on prediction, however reasonable. How good, then, *is* the EIS (entry-into-service) aircraft? What kind of job will it do for the operators? With the support of the test results, the Concorde builders were able to give firm and positive

answers to those questions. They felt able to say, without any qualification, that the EIS aircraft would exceed the contractual performance guarantees to Air France and British Airways by a substantial margin, and would be capable of carrying a full payload over more than 80 per cent of the world's supersonic route sectors.

Flying crew comfort and convenience

Safety has, of course, been a vital consideration throughout the designing and testing of Concorde. It is appropriate to start with the human element, the flight crew. Nowhere has the collaboration of the airlines been more valuable than in the design and layout of the flight deck, which embodies the practical experience and advice of airline operators and pilots.

It is designed for operation by a crew of three: pilot, co-pilot, and a third crew member who is responsible for management of the aircraft systems. Throughout, the design aim has been to avoid any unnecessary departure from standard practice. The result is that flight crews feel immediately at home in the Concorde flight deck. Pilots' control columns are conventional in type and the general arrangement of the pilots' instruments and controls is similar to that in modern subsonic transports. Most of the instruments are familiar in their presentation, and the comparatively few new instruments are clear and easy to interpret.

To ease the workload of the flight crew, a full range of automatic flight systems is installed. The aircraft has two integrated autopilot-flight director systems, auto-stabilisation, two auto-throttle systems, two independent air data systems and automatic landing facilities. An autopilot is, of course, a familiar feature but the flight director is a new equipment which computes, and directs the aircraft to follow, the ideal flight path for take-off and ascent, taking into account all the relevant factors.

Auto-stabilisation enhances the natural stability of the aircraft, and so improves pilot control and passenger comfort. It smooths out the effects of air turbulence and should there be an engine failure, the system counters any tendency by the aircraft to yaw. However, even with the auto-stabilisation system put out of action, the aircraft can be flown and controlled with ease. In flight testing, it will be recalled, Concorde has many times simulated the failure of two engines on the same side of the aircraft up to speeds of Mach 2, showing that the yaw effect can be readily controlled, with and without auto-stabilisation.

Concorde's navigation and communications system makes use of the most modern, and yet well-proven, equipment. A design requirement was that the aircraft must be capable of operation by two pilots without a navigator, and that the navigation system should enable the aircraft to fly anywhere in the world, with or without external aid.

The good visibility from Concorde's flight deck is evident in this photograph, taken as the aircraft was on its landing approach. The inset pictures show (left) one of the pilots "punching in" course co-ordinates on one of the three Inertial Navigation Systems (INS) before take-off, and (right) the flight engineer's panel from which the third member of the flight crew carries out his important task of systems management.

By the spring of 1975, the first stage of the fatigue test programme on the full-size Concorde airframe specimen in the Royal Aircraft Establishment structures laboratory at Farnborough had been completed. A total of well over 8,000 flight cycles, equivalent to more than 18,000 flying hours, had been recorded and the subsequent inspection revealed *no* defects of any significance. Testing has been resumed and it is planned to continue up to a total of at least 48,000 flight cycles at a rate that will mean that the "life" achieved by the specimen is always three times as great as that of the first aircraft to go into passenger service.

Accident statistics show that take-off and the approach to land and touch-down are the most critical phases of the flight cycle, and Concorde has several built-in advantages at these times. Its power-to-weight ratio is higher than that of subsonic aircraft and this additional reserve of power is an important safety factor at take-off. The extra lift provided naturally by the air vortex formations over the wing at landing and take-off has already been mentioned and the fact that all mechanical high-lift devices (with their inherent liability to mechanical failure) can be dispensed with is another major "plus point." In the final phase of landing, the triangular wing compresses the air beneath, producing what is called the "ground cushion effect," another helpful feature.

In the course of years of ground testing and in thousands of hours of flight testing, the structural integrity of the Concorde airframe has been thoroughly proven. In many of the ground and flight tests, the structure has been deliberately subjected to loads far exceeding anything that would be encountered in actual operations.

Hydraulic power is used in Concorde for all the aircraft services in which a rapid and certain response to control movements is essential. These services include: flying control surfaces, landing gear, wheel brakes, nosewheel steering, visor, droop nose, the moving surfaces in the engine air intakes and the transfer pumps in the fuel system. There are three completely independent hydraulic power supply systems, with the Blue and the Green systems as the normal sources of supply and the Yellow system as the standby.

Particular attention has been paid in the system design to the maintenance of essential services in emergency. The failure of any two engines would still allow two of the three systems to be operated, and even the extremely unlikely event of a failure of all four engines has been provided for. Windmilling of the engines in glide descent from high altitude will provide sufficient hydraulic power for control of the aircraft to be maintained. If engine relight has not been obtained by the time the aircraft reaches a lower altitude, the emergency power unit will provide essential hydraulic power for aircraft control.

Environmental scares
There is not space to deal with all the safety devices built into Concorde. It is, however, worth mentioning two high-altitude environmental factors, cosmic radiation and ozone, which have sometimes been thought to present a potential health hazard. There are two types of cosmic radiation, galactic and solar. The infinitesimal amount of galactic radiation absorbed by supersonic passengers flying at higher altitudes is, because of the faster flight, actually less than that absorbed by subsonic passengers flying the same route.

Solar radiation is associated with solar flare, which occurs over a well-established cycle. Nevertheless, a radiation warning meter is installed on the flight deck, and, when this gives warning of a sudden increase in radiation intensity, the aircraft will descend to a lower altitude and continue its journey subsonically. Records show that this would have been necessary only five times in the last 39 years.

Ozone is a toxic gas, and it is present in measurable quantities in the atmosphere at the Concorde cruise altitude. There were fears that the cabin air supplied to the passengers would be contaminated by ozone since it is tapped from the engines which draw their air from the ambient atmosphere. However, any ozone present in the intake air is destroyed by the high temperature at which the engines operate, and in many tests simulating high-altitude operating conditions it has proved impossible to introduce any trace of ozone into the cabin. But again, to provide a safeguard, an ozone filter is fitted in the cabin air supply system.

The years Concorde has been under development have seen a world-wide growth in concern about the environment. Supersonic flight has inevitably been one of the targets. It has been possible to dismiss some of the scare stories – that passengers would have to remain seated, and that, because of cosmic radiation, we should be served only by stewardesses over child-bearing age – as the fantasies they were.

Opposite: Operations from overseas airports such as Los Angeles have demonstrated the ease with which Concorde can be serviced. Below: Main servicing points on the aircraft.

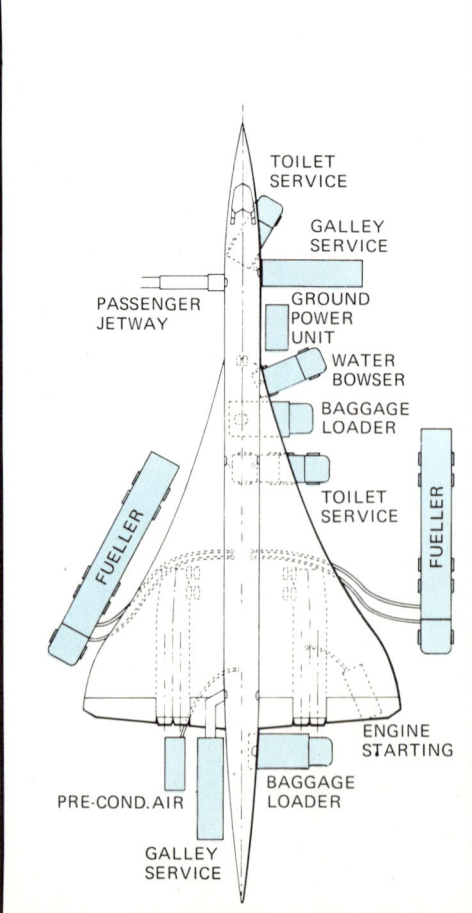

TOILET SERVICE

GALLEY SERVICE

PASSENGER JETWAY

GROUND POWER UNIT

WATER BOWSER

BAGGAGE LOADER

TOILET SERVICE

FUELLER

FUELLER

ENGINE STARTING

PRE-COND. AIR

BAGGAGE LOADER

GALLEY SERVICE

The sonic boom
Sonic boom is a phenomenon inseparable from supersonic flight. Once an aircraft begins to exceed a speed of about Mach 1.15 (about 850mph), its shock waves start to reach the ground and a sonic boom is created. The sound can be heard across a corridor of up to 50 miles wide, the intensity being highest directly under the flight path of the aircraft but dying away to a faint rumble towards the edges of the corridor.

Because of its suddenness, sonic boom has a startling effect, especially when it is first experienced. Concorde's sonic boom will not cause physical damage to human beings or animals and the average "overpressure" (the sudden rise and fall in temperature at ground level) of about 1½lb. per square foot will not cause material damage to any structure in a reasonable state of repair. (To relate that overpressure to something in normal everyday experience, one can say that it is equivalent to the pressure one would feel when putting a hand out of the window of a car travelling at 30mph.)

It will be for individual governments to decide whether supersonic airliner operations can be permitted along carefully defined corridors through their national airspace. In some areas of the world, notably the Middle East, South America and Australia, supersonic corridors have been temporarily created in order that governments could assess the boom and test public reaction to it. Over oceans, sonic boom presents no problem. It has no effect on marine life, and in the course of Concorde's tours, many thousands of vessels of all sizes and types have been overflown without any adverse reports ever having been received.

Contrary to one popular misconception, there will also be no sonic boom problem in the locality of airports served by Concorde; in these localities, Concorde is a subsonic aircraft. After taking off, it will fly for about 100 miles before it reaches a speed at which it would start to create a boom, and at the other end of the journey it will be decelerating to a "non-boom" speed when it is still about 100 miles from its destination airport. Flight planning will also be so arranged as to place the acceleration boom over the sea or over a sparsely populated area.

Airport pollution
Airfield noise is admittedly a more difficult problem. It is not possible to use a high bypass-ratio engine (a turbofan) in a supersonic airliner because the large frontal area of such engines would create unacceptable drag at supersonic speed. In the present state of the art, therefore, there is little prospect of making the Concorde engines as quiet as those of the second-generation subsonic jets. This is not to say, however, that Concorde's airfield noise levels will be obtrusive.

When at the time of the 1972 world tour, the early-development Olympus 593 engines in the prototype Concorde 002 were criticised as noisy, the airframe and aero-engine manufacturers stated that at entry into service the airfield noise levels of Concorde would be comparable with those of such well-known subsonic jets as the 707, the DC 8 and the VC 10. It was pointed out that many hundreds of these aircraft will continue in front-line service for many years after Concorde has started operation.

This forecast on noise levels has been made good. Measurements of engine noise

in the approach, in fly-over and to the side of the runway are made at internationally agreed recording points, and independent measurements have confirmed the manufacturers' predictions. Concorde's overall airfield noise levels are in the same "ballpark" as those of the first-generation subsonic jets, marginally worse in some respects and marginally better in others. In a series of test flights at Casablanca airport, Concorde demonstrated its ability to meet the stringent noise restrictions in force at J.F. Kennedy airport, New York.

The statement that Concorde's noise will not stand out from the general pattern of airport operations is borne out by experience on its overseas tours, during which it has visited some seventy airports in forty different countries. Concorde has flown into and out of these airports without arousing any special concern, despite the attempts of many local environmental groups to organise opposition to it.

Another charge laid against Concorde is that it will seriously increase ground level pollution at airports. The basis of this charge seems to be that when the aircraft is taxying, the level of carbon monoxide emission from its engines is slightly higher than that from subsonic aircraft engines. But within the airport complex, by far the greater amount of carbon monoxide comes not from aircraft, but from the fleets of ground servicing vehicles.

Stratospheric bogies
The most emotional and, in some ways, most damaging accusations levelled at supersonic airliners by the environmentalists have been concerned with stratospheric effects of high-altitude flying. Much of the emotion whipped up against the American SST – which provided the popular political support for its cancellation – was based on "scientific" theories which have since been shown to have been wildly exaggerated.

Ozone depletion is now the fashionable charge, but in the earlier years, there were other stratospheric bogies. There were suggestions that water vapour in the engine exhausts would create a permanent cloud barrier at high altitude flying, but there was no general agreement on what the result would be; one school forecast that the cloud layer would cut off much of the sun's heat and so bring about a new ice age on earth, and the opposite view was that the layer would create a "greenhouse" effect and send ground temperatures soaring.

These theories have now been discredited, but at the time they were first put forward they attracted worldwide attention. They were based on inadequate knowledge of the atmospheric circulation system in the stratosphere and they overlooked, or deliberately ignored, the fact that vast amounts of water vapour, far exceeding anything that could be produced by hundreds of aircraft, are daily injected into the stratosphere by tropical thunderstorms and other natural phenomena.

The main point of attack has now shifted to the alleged threat posed by Concorde to the ozone layer in the stratosphere. Opponents of SSTs allege that the nitrous oxides in the engine exhausts will partially erode the ozone layer, allowing a higher intensity of ultra-violet radiation to penetrate to the earth's surface and so cause an increased incidence of skin cancer.

The most comprehensive programme of research into the possible effects of stratospheric pollution by aircraft is the Climatic Impact Assessment Programme (CIAP) mounted by the US Department of Transportation. This involved a number of other government departments and agencies in the USA and other countries and drew on the talents of 1,000 investigators in many American and foreign universities.

In the report of the CIAP findings, one of the principal conclusions was that operations of present-day supersonic airliners and those currently scheduled to enter service would cause climatic effects which are much smaller than those minimally detectable. This minimum detectable change in global mean ozone was estimated by the Department of Transportation to be 0.5 per cent, and 100 Concordes each operating in the stratosphere for up to four and a half hours every day would have less than this effect. To set this minimum detectable change in perspective, the report pointed out that the natural fluctuation over Washington, DC, is 25 per cent and that there is a natural variation of as much as 30 per cent between Texas and Minnesota.

Fuel consumption
At a press conference to introduce the report, the director of the CIAP study project, Dr Alan Grobecker, described the SST as "merely a pimple" on the overall environmental problem compared with other sources of pollution. When asked to relate the 0.5 per cent reduction in ozone to skin cancer, Dr Grobecker said that this was the equivalent of 45 minutes on the beach.

One last accusation against Concorde remains to be answered. It is claimed that it will greatly hasten the rate at which the world's oil fuel resources are used up, and the rider is always added that this is happening merely to save businessmen a few hours' flying time. This criticism will not stand up to examination.

Admittedly, Concorde's fuel consumption is higher than that of current subsonic jets but the effect of this, against the world background, is negligible. The total consumption of oil fuel by civil aviation amounts to not more than six per cent of world consumption and on the most optimistic market estimates Concorde cannot be expected to take more than eight per cent of the total world air passenger market.

This would mean that Concorde would add rather less than 0.5 per cent to total world oil consumption. A small enough figure, but how does one make it comprehensible to the ordinary motorist? One way would be to say that if there are 30 years reserves of fuel left on earth, 100 Concordes operating daily throughout that period would shorten the 30 years by 20 days. So we need to look elsewhere for major savings in oil fuel, and ultimately, of course, we need to look to much-maligned technology to develop alternative sources of energy well before we run out of oil.

Counting the cost
And what has it all cost? In 1962 the total bill was expected to be between £150 million and £170 million. In December, 1974, a written Parliamentary answer gave the information that the cost to Britain and France of developing Concorde up to the point at which it will enter airline service was then estimated to be £974 million. The three main factors responsible for this sixfold increase are inflation, currency devaluation and design changes.

Inflation and devaluation have, in fact, been responsible for about 45 per cent of the increase. But why did the people who launched the project get the other costs so mistaken? The straight answer must be: "They would have needed to be superhuman to get them right." These men were trying to do something that had never been done before – build an aeroplane that would carry 100 passengers at twice the speed of sound – and they had no precedents for designing and marketing a supersonic airliner. The men in charge did not, and could not, know what a jungle of problems they would have to hack their way through.

To look at it another way, Britain has invested, over 12 years, £40 million a year in Concorde. This is not a large sum when you compare it with the money paid by the British government to bail out collapsing industrial firms.

In straight accountancy terms, there will probably be no direct recovery of any part of the Concorde research and development costs. They must be regarded as part of our national investment in the future, part of the price we need to pay to retain our competitive position in a world where every nation is striving to achieve industrial self-sufficiency.

The demands of the Concorde programme have pushed forward the frontiers of knowledge, not only in the aerospace industry, but also in a number of other advanced-technology industries which have been called upon to provide supplies or services for the project. New managerial skills have been acquired, the use of computers in design and production applications have been greatly extended, new types of machine tools and new manufacturing techniques have been developed, and advances have been made in the technology of paints, glass, plastics, and non-ferrous metals – all because of Concorde. As a result of the spur to product improvement provided by Concorde, millions of pounds' worth of export business has been gained by British firms.

Until now, the Concorde story has been one of heavy financial outgoings, the only offset being in the somewhat indefinite area of spin-off. The extent to which Concorde will in the future make a measurable financial return to Britain depends on the level of overseas sales it achieves.

Export earnings
British Airways will soon start to earn useful sums of foreign currency from the sale of Concorde seats, but the real benefit to Britain's balance of payments will begin to accrue only after Concorde enters service with foreign operators. Every sale to an overseas airline would mean a substantial boost to this country's export earnings, not merely from the initial sale but from the continuing revenue derived throughout the aircraft's operating life, from overhauls, spares, and other product support activities. A relatively modest total sale of 50 aircraft overseas would bring in hundreds of millions of pounds over the next two decades.

But in reality it is far too early to strike any true balance. We have, in the development of air transport, almost certainly reached a "speed plateau" with Concorde.

An unusual view of Concorde seen in flight, showing the elegance of its delta-wing shape to great advantage. It is in the colours of Air France.

WAY AHEAD

The year 1976 will be the first of a new era of air transport. In the Western World, British Airways and Air France will inaugurate the supersonic age with Concorde services between London and Bahrain and between Paris and Rio de Janeiro. In Russia the TU 144 will enter service with Aeroflot.

Are we justified in saying that Concorde will introduce a "new" era in transport? New eras in transport have begun whenever a new type of vehicle has made travel markedly more convenient and comfortable, and that has always included making it faster. In their day, the railway train, the steamship and the first airliners all fulfilled this requirement. It was not so much that they opened up new routes as that they made the established routes easier going for the traveller.

Measured by that yardstick, the subsonic jetliner itself can be said to have ushered in a new transport age, Concorde's performance "edge" over the subsonic jets is greater than the one they enjoyed over their predecessors. Concorde passengers will find that supersonic speed opens up entirely new possibilities of efficient and relaxed intercontinental travel.

It is an experience that cannot be fully appreciated until it has been lived through, and only then if the passenger has some first-hand knowledge of long-distance air journeys. To be told or to read that Concorde cuts three hours off a six-hour subsonic flight time makes an impact, but the full impact of that time-saving can be felt only by making the flight in Concorde.

Travel boredom and fatigue

For the average air traveller who flies regularly on business, a trip of three hours' duration is just about the limit before boredom begins to set in. In three hours, he has had a drink and an unhurried meal, he has looked through his papers and made some notes. Then he realises that he is only half-way on his journey, and the boredom curve begins to rise. Those next three hours seem twice as long as the first three. A good in-flight film can help to pass the time, but there does not appear to be enough good

An air-to-air photograph of the production-standard Concorde in the livery of British Airways. Insert: Its passenger cabin.

A little-recognised role of the manufacturers' test pilots is training of airline crews. BAC's Director of Flight Test, Brian Trubshaw, is seen (right) during a training flight with a senior British Airways pilot.

films to go round. Boredom is not a particularly tragic state, but it is depressing and is a factor in fatigue.

On the longest Concorde route sector, the passenger will find that at the end of those first three "tolerable" hours, the aircraft is starting on its descent to land. The boredom factor will hardly have had time to come into operation. It is now, as the stewardess makes her arrival announcement and the passenger adjusts his watch to local time, that the supersonic message gets through. One has seen this happen scores of time when greeting passengers disembarking from Concorde demonstration flights.

Many of them have gone aboard prepared to admit that the Concorde looks a beautiful aeroplane but otherwise in what the Scots would call a "canny" mood. During the flight they duly made the polite noises: praised the smoothness and calm of supersonic travel and, on occasions, applauded the Machmeter for registering Mach 2. But the reaction on arrival is something quite different from mere politeness. When the fact of the time-saving hits home, when they realise that if they had travelled by subsonic aircraft they would still be several hours away, a common comment is: "This has spoiled me for flying the old way."

Jet lag

In referring to boredom and fatigue, we have been speaking of average subjective reactions, and we accept that there are wide variations in individual tolerance of these factors. Some people find a long flight totally exhausting and take several days to recover; other people are "bright-eyed and bushy-tailed" after a few hours of sleep on arrival. There are several scientifically-based methods of measuring the amount of recovery time that the normal passenger requires after a long flight. The best-known – the ICAO formula – takes account of four factors: the length of the flight, the number of time zones crossed on route, the time of day at departure and the time of day at arrival.

A considerable saving in passenger re-

covery time is indicated when this formula is applied to Concorde operations on typical routes. This saving derives not only from the shorter journey time, but from the improved scheduling flexibility that supersonic cruise speed allows. Schedules can usually be so arranged as to avoid arrivals and departures late at night or in the small hours of the morning. Services from Los Angeles to Melbourne or from Melbourne to London could be scheduled so as to save the Concorde passengers two days recovery time, a saving that, for the business executive, would far outweigh the extra fare.

Commuting by Concorde

By making it less exhausting and time-consuming, Concorde will encourage more business travel. For the first time, a day return trip will become practicable between a number of the world's "big city pairs," such as London or Paris and New York; Tokyo and Hong Kong; and San Francisco and Mexico City. This kind of day return trip is not just a gimmick; a businessman in any of these cities will be able to travel to the "city pair", do several hours of work, and be back in his own bed before midnight without ever moving out of his normal bodily rhythm.

Even if a businessman does not want to compress his Transatlantic sorties into one day, he can still take advantage of the

Above: Concorde at Melbourne's new Tullamarine Airport during the "endurance flying" programme in the summer of 1975. Opposite: Concorde, the first of a new breed of airliners which is halving the world in size, opening up a new era in transport, one of easier and speedier communication.

greater flexibility of supersonic operations. To illustrate that point, consider the scope for improving the service from New York to Europe. At present, because of airport curfews at both ends of the journey, flights to Europe can be scheduled from New York only up to about 10 a.m. and from late afternoon onward. Concorde's greater speed will enable it to be scheduled for departure time from New York up to about 2 p.m. Today, it is only travellers in the Eastern states who can catch a 7 a.m. departure from their own city and make a connection in New York for a same-day arrival in Europe. Concorde's later departure times will extend this facility to cover about two-thirds of the USA.

To put the matter quite simply, supersonic travel is better travel. It will cost more, but for those passengers whose time means money, it will be better value. Nor does one need to apologise for the fact that, at first, supersonic service will be an élitist form of travel. Middle-aged people

today have seen the subsonic airliner develop from a transport vehicle for the privileged few into an essential component of the mass-market package-tour holiday.

Concorde's future development will follow the same trend. It may take a long time for supersonic travel to become the standard form of air transport but, sooner or later, this will happen. When there is a better product available, even at a higher price, most people will want it, and more and more people will contrive to have it.

In the supersonic age, this will be a smaller, more closely-knit world. Scarcely any two major cities anywhere on earth will be more than a 12-hour Concorde flight apart. Two cities which will be an exception to this rule are Melbourne and London, but even they will be less than 14 hours distant from each other. No continent will gain more from the supersonic speeding-up of international communications than Australia, separated as it is by vast distances from the rest of the world.

The shrinking world

Whenever in the past it has become possible for the first time to complete a journey within 12 hours – a working day – the volume of traffic on that route has started to expand. On the North Atlantic crossing, jet-powered airliners were the first to break through the 12-hour barrier, and this was without doubt the main reason for the upsurge in traffic that occurred on these routes in the early 1960s.

What the subsonic jets did for the North Atlantic, Concorde will do for the Trans-Pacific routes. Clearly, its time-savings between Europe and North America will have great passenger appeal, but it is over the long route sectors of the Pacific that the supersonic airliner will come into its own.

The rate of industrial and economic expansion in the Pacific basin has in recent years probably exceeded that in any other part of the world and although the rate may decelerate, growth will continue. Prospects for Pacific business and Pacific travel rest mainly on three firm bases – the American West Coast, Japan and Australia. The increasing interdependence of the three areas is reflected in the growing air traffic between them, and as much of this is business traffic Concorde will achieve a substantial market penetration.

Furthermore, there will be few sonic boom restrictions to curtail Concorde's time-savings over the long Pacific routes. Most of the international airports in the Pacific area are situated either on islands or near continental coastlines, and on the great majority of Concorde route sectors the aircraft can be routed to fly almost the whole journey over the sea.

In the end, we come back to the basic point that the supersonic age inaugurated by Concorde *will* be a new era in transport, an era of easier and speedier world communication that will benefit everyone. Concorde is the first of a new breed of airliners. Without harming the world environment, it will set new standards of travel comfort and efficiency. Once these standards have been set, the travelling public will insist on their being maintained and improved. There will be derivatives of Concorde, possibly produced in co-operation between Europe and the United States.

But, meantime, Concorde stands poised to go into airline service – and stands poised for success.